PRAISE FOR

STAY HERE: ON LOVE, LOSS, AND REMAINING

BY KAREN GOLDFINGER BAKER

...

"*Stay Here* is a rare kind of book—honest, spacious, and deeply human. Karen Goldfinger Baker doesn't try to fix grief or package it into tidy lessons. Instead, she sits beside it and invites us to do the same. These pages feel like quiet companionship for anyone who has loved and lost. A beautiful reminder that even in the ache, love remains."

—JACOB NORDBY, AUTHOR OF *THE CREATIVE CURE: HOW FINDING AND FREEING YOUR INNER ARTIST CAN HEAL YOUR LIFE*

"We spend so much of our lives trying to avoid or fix what we feel. Through the lens of grief, Karen Goldfinger Baker shows that healing doesn't come from moving on or toughing it out, but by being with what is. *Stay Here* is brutally honest and exquisitely beautiful and reminds us of something most of us have forgotten: The capacity to stay is the capacity to love."

—MARK J. SILVERMAN, AUTHOR OF *THE RISING LEADER HANDBOOK: TURNING HIGH ACHIEVERS INTO EFFECTIVE LEADERS*

"*Stay Here* is a gift. As someone who proudly talks about my 'many dead friends'—and has a Protector Area in my home dedicated to all of them—I appreciate deeply any honest and raw exploration around grief.

Karen Goldfinger Baker does not shy away from the visceral experience of loving and losing someone precious. She is able to translate the indescribable into the relatable. And, when we are on our knees, without words or even breath, she gives us something to hold onto. Grateful for her courage and tenacity and all-out realness. *Stay Here* is a book to keep and also to share."

—REV. RACHEL HOLLANDER, AUTHOR OF *FROM THERE TO HERE: AN INSIDER'S GUIDE TO NAVIGATING THE DARKNESS*

"This book not only feels beautiful to read, but it was also deeply useful to me in my own time of grieving. *Stay Here* draws you in—a series of touching poems, so light upon the soul—but it also shakes and refreshes you with hope, compassion, and true help in a time that can feel helpless."

—STEVE CHANDLER, AUTHOR OF *RIGHT NOW: MASTERING THE BEAUTY OF THE PRESENT MOMENT* AND *TIME WARRIOR*

"I'm an orphan too. It is a waymarker that, once passed, the ground won't allow our footsteps to be erased by time or any natural force. Without parents, I will always be without the epithet of 'his daughter' or 'her youngest' after my name. I am less and also more for being theirs.

Grief is impatient and impolite. The discomfort it carves is exactly the shape and size of the joy that loving people, animals, and places once filled us with—sunflower yellow and irrepressible, before it diluted to an ache.

Karen Goldfinger Baker's blue is her mother's eyes. I know something about that. In *Loving Large*, I wrote about my father, my lighthouse, and my blue eyes as weak consolation. Now, I celebrate his eyes in my grandson's miraculous face. Baker's Toby and David are her blue. Yet, they are every person, creature, and place we cast on, gaze on in the last moments of knowing them. When the smile fades, the space it leaves is not empty. It is the precise measurement of how much we loved.

Stay Here does not ask you to heal. We never do. It invites us to choose our blue, while remembering the colors that once filled the space in our broken hearts."

—PATTI M. HALL, AUTHOR OF *LOVING LARGE: A MOTHER'S RARE DISEASE MEMOIR*

"We spend so much of our lives trying to move past what hurts. *Stay Here* interrupts that. Karen Goldfinger Baker invites a different relationship with grief—not avoidance, but presence. This book isn't just about loss. It's about being fully alive."

—JASON GOLDBERG, AUTHOR OF *PRISON BREAK: VANQUISH THE VICTIM, OWN YOUR OBSTACLES, AND LEAD YOUR LIFE*

"It's hard to capture in a few words how profoundly moving this book is. I devoured *Stay Here* as a witness and a mirror to my own grieving process with the recent loss of my mother. Karen Goldfinger Baker's words echo so many mundane and sacred thoughts I had, and still have, in my walk with death and grief, (like wondering for the nine billionth time, whether we said enough to my mom while keeping vigil until the end). Loss is part of living and loving, but we just don't know how to do grief, or be with grief. *Stay Here* is a book for all humans, a beautiful guide for anyone navigating grief and loss, or for supporting someone through that journey. "

"'Life is what happens to you while you're busy making other plans,' John Lennon once sang. This is the book written for that moment—for the times when you find yourself on a path you never meant to take, carrying questions with no clear answers. *Stay Here* doesn't ask you to fix or flee what hurts. Instead, it invites you to sit beside it. To listen. To soften toward your own pain.

You won't find instructions here—there are plenty of books that try to do that already. What you'll find instead is gentle companionship, a quiet space to breathe, and a way to make room for tenderness amid loss. *Stay here*. You are not alone.

Please, do yourself the kindness of reading this book—it touches a part of the human experience that eventually reaches us all."

stay here

ON LOVE, LOSS, AND REMAINING

KAREN GOLDFINGER BAKER

Compassionate Mind
Collaborative

cmcollab.com

Published by Compassionate Mind Collaborative

**Compassionate Mind
Collaborative**

cmcollab.com

Edited by Heather Doyle Fraser
Cover and interior design and layout by Cindy Curtis-Rivera
Proofed by Hope Madden
Marketing by Jesse Sussman
Author Photo by David Baker

ISBN 979-8-9957755-0-8 (paperback)
ISBN 979-8-9957755-1-5 (ebook)

This paperback edition first published in 2026.

contents

four

THE THING ABOUT GRIEF IS… IT'S A SILENT WATCHER

five

THE THING ABOUT GRIEF IS… NOTHING IS EVER THE SAME

six

THE THING ABOUT GRIEF IS… IT LIVES WITH YOU

seven

THE THING ABOUT GRIEF IS… I CAN MAKE PEACE WITH IT

epilogue

acknowledgments

about the author

dedication

For those I love who are no longer here: you are the reason I stayed, the reason I write for anyone learning to live with what is no longer there.

prologue

ONE JOURNEY CHOOSES US

This is the book that wasn't there when I needed it.
The book I went looking for and couldn't find.
The book I wanted to read.

So I wrote it.

And just maybe, it's a book for you, too,
if you have found yourself taking a journey to somewhere
you never meant to go.
This journey chooses you.

The road is bumpy and disorienting.
The language feels foreign.
We don't always know how to ask for what we need.
And even when we do, what arrives rarely looks the way
we imagined.

Still, it is a journey.

We cannot control the terrain.
We can look for peace.
We can decide what we carry forward.
We can learn the rhythm of our own surrender.

We change.

This book is not here to rush us.
It is not here to fix us.
It is here to sit beside us.

Grief asks us to go places we never wanted to see.
It takes us somewhere we did not choose.

But healing—if it comes—begins somewhere quieter.

It begins when we stop trying to outrun the ache,
When we stop demanding a different map,
When we allow absence to have presence,
When we let love exist in the same space as loss.

We do not have to solve this.
We do not have to escape it.

Stay here.
Even here.
Especially here.

one

THE THING ABOUT GRIEF IS...

it's hard

I'm going to let you in on a secret about grief at the very beginning.

Here's what I want you to know: the hard part of grief is the whole thing.

All of it.

And I also want you to know this: the whole thing is beautiful.

And hard.

meet my mom: joyful toby

For me, my mother was brilliance. She was independence. Generosity.

Laser-focused truth that could take you down at the knees if you weren't ready.

She had a vertical presence.

Even when I grew up, I never stopped looking up.

She was smart and well-read. Books were not decoration in our house—they were currency, compass, oxygen. She loved card games and travel, the kind that stretched you and the kind that wrapped you in luxury. She believed women should gather, collaborate, build something together.

From her I learned:

That leaving home will break your heart and expand it in equal measure.

That any tradition that makes a girl smaller deserves to be questioned.

That reading is not a hobby—it's a roadmap.

That if the roadmap points somewhere wild, you go.

Send your kids to camp. Even the youngest one. Especially the youngest one.

Buy inexpensive clothes, but never cheap shoes.

If you want community, host the party. (A keg of Genesee helps.)

When a room feels too tight, knock down the wall. The box is not sacred. The sledgehammer is not destruction—it's possibility.

And if no one claims the towel at lost and found, claim it. It's not stealing. It's opportunity.

She said outrageous things. She held strong opinions. She did not suffer fools.

And she trusted me.

She trusted me to fight for her life when it mattered.
And to advocate for her death when that mattered more.

What I learned last—what I learned in the quiet spaces when it was just us—is that the woman many people called "a tough broad" was soft at the center. Connected. Tender. Capable of deep vulnerability at the intersection of motherhood and daughterhood and loyalty and love.

I stand with her at that intersection.

The pavement there isn't gold because it's shiny.
It's gold because it's sacred.

go so you can come back

"Go so you can come back."
Seriously.
Who says something like that?

My mother did.
Every time I left.

Out the door for school.
Out the door for a date.
Out the door for a new experience, a new chapter in life.

"Go so you can come back."

It felt controlling. Circular. Nonsensical.
I wanted to go without the return built in.
I wanted independence without the tether.

I rolled my eyes.
It took her dying for me to understand.
She was blessing the leaving.

Go.
Stretch.
Risk.
Live wide.

And also—
come back.

Return safely.
Let me see your face again.
Let me know the world did not swallow you whole.

It was never about geography.
It was about continuity.
About love that expected movement and still hoped for
return.

After she was gone, I began to hear it differently.

Now, when someone I love walks out the door,
when a call ends,
when headlights disappear down the street,
I feel the echo of it rise in my chest.

Go so you can come back.

Not a command.
Not a leash.

A blessing disguised as a sentence.

Love doesn't always announce itself as love.
Sometimes it hides in repetition.
In ordinary language.
In the things we think are dumb until it's too late to ask
for them again.

meet my dad: david goldfinger was a poet

I can still feel the brown paper bag in my hand as I walked into the cafeteria.

I don't remember what was inside.
I'm not even sure I liked what he packed.

It didn't matter.
What mattered was the outside.

Every day of my senior year of high school, my dad made my lunch. Not because he had to. Not because my mom couldn't. He did it because he wanted to. And every single day, five days a week, he wrote a poem on the front of the bag.

Each one began the same way:
Karen G—

And no matter what clever or ridiculous middle he came up with, they always ended with something like:
"a friend to me"
or
"I love thee."

My dad was a mediocre poet at best.

The rhymes were predictable. The meter, questionable.
But his commitment? Relentless.

He was playful that way. Funny. Unapologetically
sentimental. A successful, driven, strong man—the kind
who built things, who led, who achieved—and still took
the time to write dorky poems on a brown paper bag for
his teenage daughter.

He didn't write them for the world.
He wrote them for me.
And for my friends, who would gather around my lunch
table to see what Goldfinger had written that day.

That was my dad.
Strong. Driven. Fiercely loyal.
And soft in all the right places.

At the end, his body was failing him.
His heart was tired. His circulation slowed. The man who
had powered through life on force of will alone could not
will this away.

In the dark one night, he turned his head toward me and,
in a voice thin and frayed, said, "You are a loving person…"

I fell apart. Tears. Snot. The kind of crying that comes
from somewhere ancient.

In his way—practical, understated, exact—he was finishing something. Offering gratitude. Naming what he saw. The strong man who had spent a lifetime achieving and pushing and building chose, at the end, to give me that.

And for all of his strength, all of his drive, all of the ways he did not go gently—his greatest act of strength was this: He let go.

true confession

Some days in the ecosystem of hospice are hard.

Dad is comfortable.
Breathing—shallow, but steady.
Not in pain.

By all visible measures, it is a good day.
I am the one unraveling.

I can't get out of my own way. The people I love most feel like sandpaper against my skin. Their kindness irritates me. Their questions exhaust me. Even their presence feels loud.

I cannot find the spaciousness I usually pride myself on—the place where I forgive easily, let things slide, offer grace.

There is no grace in me.

I want a real meal, something warm and grounding, but when food is in front of me, my appetite disappears. My body is confused. My nervous system doesn't know whether to sit vigil or flee.

I am carrying everything at once—stress, confusion, sadness, anger, relief—packed tight beneath my shoulder blade like a clenched fist. It aches. Not dramatically. Just persistently. A small, private throb.

Part of me wants to disappear. To be somewhere quiet and wind-swept. An island, maybe. Mostly alone. My dog at my feet. My husband close enough to love, far enough to not need anything from me.

I am tired in a way that sleep won't fix.
Foggy. Thin-skinned.

And beneath it all, the quiet shame:
How can I be so wrapped up in myself while my father's life is slowly loosening its grip?
But this, too, is part of hospice.

The body in the bed.
The body keeping watch.
Both breaking in different ways.

time of death

Pay attention to the clock.
That's what the hospice nurses said.
Not poetically. Practically.

Every two hours.
Every four.
Write it down.
Stay ahead of the pain.

Morphine has a rhythm.
Ativan has a window.
Breath has a pattern until it doesn't.

Pay attention to the clock.

Labored breathing has a way of swallowing the room.
It pulls your eyes to the rise and fall, the pause, the space between.
Final breaths melt everything else into background noise—
the lamp, the hallway, the person whispering in the kitchen.

The clock on the wall keeps ticking, but it no longer feels like time.
It feels like instruction.

Pay attention.

For days, time had already been bending.
There was the before—ordinary mornings, coffee, errands.
Then there was this strange in-between—normal life continuing at the edges, while a hospital bed sat in the room that already had a big, comfortable bed. Schedules layered on top of decline. Medication charts next to grocery lists.

Pay attention to the clock.

Because when the breathing stops, something else does too.

The nurses knew this.
That someone would need to mark it.
That someone would have to look up, find the hands, name the minute.

The clock does not actually stop.
It keeps moving.

But there is a tick—a single, ordinary tick—that divides a life into pieces.

Before that sound.
After it.
Pay attention to the clock.
Tick.

wisdom

We do the best we can.

adrift

It happened quietly.
One day I had parents.
And then I didn't.

There is no ceremony for becoming parentless. No announcement. Just an absence that rearranges the room.

For most of my life, I could say, "I'm going to my parents' house." Even as an adult. Even with gray threading through my hair. There was still a place where I was someone's child.
Now there isn't.

I used to feel a certain ache when I met people who had lost both parents. I could see the vacancy around them. No one left who remembered them before they remembered themselves. No one to call and ask, "Was I always like this?"

I understand that ache differently now.
Parents ground us in our past.

They hold the early versions of us—the gap-toothed smiles, the slammed doors, the awkward middle school years, the first brave steps into the world. They remember the stories we have forgotten. They correct our timelines. They laugh at things no one else witnessed.

When one parent dies, you are still someone's child. There is still a living bridge back to where you began.
When the second one dies, something else shifts.
The bridge lifts.

I am still their daughter. That does not change. But there is no longer anyone alive who stood in the kitchen when I was seven. No one who watched me leave for college. No one who can say my childhood nickname with the same ease.

Losing both of them did not make me an orphan in the literal sense.
But it did set me adrift in time.
It is a quiet dislocation. A subtle untethering. I move forward like everyone else, but the root system has changed.
It may look like I've moved on.
I have not.
I carry them differently now.

Not as a place I can return to,
but as the ground beneath me.

irrevocably altered

There's no returning to my former self.
There are those who wait for me to come back.
But I am changed.
I don't yet know who I am becoming, but this I know:
the old me died that day, too.

the love that remains

People will tell you to be strong.
They said it to me in waiting rooms and grocery store aisles. They said it softly, as if strength were something I could put on like a coat.
What they meant was: survive this.
What I learned is that survival doesn't feel like strength. It feels like standing.

There were days I could not solve another problem. Not another medication change. Not another explanation of her health history. I could not research one more option or debate one more strategy.

The charts and binders sat open on the kitchen table. My phone buzzed with questions.
And still, there were moments when none of that mattered.
There is a particular loneliness in reaching for a hand that isn't reaching back.

There is a particular kind of negotiation that happens between necessity and dignity. How much help is too much? When does assistance become exposure? I watched my mother's anger flare as pieces of her independence fell away. I understood it in my bones. Her whole self felt under siege.

Strength had nothing to do with it.
Love did.
My entire life, I heard my mother say my name. Across rooms. From the kitchen. On the phone. My name shaped by her mouth.
I will never hear that sound again.

Sometimes in dreams she is walking past me, saying it—not urgently, just as she always did. As if I am still hers to call.

When I wake up, there is no voice.
There is only the echo.
And what remains after the voice is gone isn't strength.
It's something more primal.

The love has moved inward.
It is no longer something I reach for or perform.
It is no longer a hand to hold or a name spoken across a room.

It is structural now.
Bone-deep.
Part of how I stand.

waiting while hating the waiting

The hardest part about hospice is the waiting.

Not the medication schedules.
Not the visitors.
Not even the visible decline.

The waiting.

It is a strange, suspended kind of time. Familiar in shape, but not in weight. Like waiting for something ordinary—a delayed flight, the coffee maker to finish, the repair technician to arrive—except nothing about this is ordinary.

And so I sat.

Waiting for the thing I did not want.
Waiting for what I knew would come.
Waiting for death.

I did not know when it would happen. No one could tell me. And so my life narrowed to the radius of the bed.

I paused everything that felt optional. Emails. Errands. Plans. I loosened my grip on my list of "shoulds," though not without resistance. It is harder than it sounds to let a day be exactly what it is.

Over and over, I reminded myself:

There isn't a problem to solve.
There is nothing to fix.
There is only comfort to offer.
Only presence.

Sometimes I believed that.
Sometimes I just repeated it like a prayer.

When I stood up—to stretch, to shower, to use the bathroom—I felt the fragile thread of it all. I worried that in the brief moment my back was turned, death would slip in quietly. That I would miss it. That the last breath would happen in my absence.

It felt irrational. And completely real.
Waiting like that rearranges you.
You begin to understand that you are not in control of the timing. You are only in control of how gently you sit beside it.
And some days, I did that well.

Other days, I was simply there.
And that had to be enough.

guilt

I could have done more.
That sentence has teeth.

It circles back in the quiet hours. It sits at the edge of memory and asks questions no one can answer.

Maybe it wasn't your time.
Maybe I hurried what would have unfolded on its own.
Maybe my steadiness was interference.

I know what the doctors said. I know what hospice is for. I know what compassion looks like on paper.

And still.

There is a particular kind of guilt that belongs to the one who stands closest to the bed. The one who nods when the plan is explained. The one who says, "Yes. Keep him comfortable." The one who understands that comfort sometimes means letting go.

From the outside, it looks like love.
From the inside, it can feel like betrayal.
Guilt is not rational. It does not care about credentials or consensus. It does not bow to reason.
It lives in the body.

It hums beneath the memory of those final days. It asks whether I leaned too far in one direction. It asks whether I should have held tighter.

And woven through it—inseparable—is love.
Not clean love. Not saintly love.
Human love.
The kind that makes impossible choices and then lies awake replaying them.
I suspect guilt softens with time. I hope it does.
But even if it doesn't disappear entirely, I know this:

It is proof that I was there.
That I cared enough to question myself.
That love and responsibility were braided together so tightly I can't always tell them apart.

All the feelings were real.
The relief.
The sorrow.
The exhaustion.
The guilt.

They belong to the same moment.

if you need anything...

They will say "If you need anything, let me know."
They will say it again.
And again.

You will hear this.
You will say "OK."
You might even say "Thank you."

Or if you are anything like me, you won't have a response.
I acknowledge the kindness in their offer.
But for me, the offer feels like abandonment.
My brain under the influence of grief is shut down under stress.
I cannot plan or ask for help.
I'm over here trying to breathe.
Trying to survive.

I don't need your offer of anything.

I need my person back.
I need to forget.
I need to remember.
I need your action.
I need your check-in.
I need ...

normal things are confusing

I'm not the person I used to be.

You would recognize me. My face hasn't changed. My voice still carries the same tone. I answer to the same name. From the outside, continuity is intact.

But the morning after my mom died, I drove to CVS.

It felt like proof that the world expected me to continue.

The sky was bright and warm—the kind of day I've always loved. I have always loved the sun. But that morning, it felt offensive. I squinted upward and thought, almost involuntarily, how can you shine like this?

How can you do what you always do when everything is not what it was?

Inside the store, the automatic voice greeted me: "Welcome to CVS."

The doors opened the way they always do.

People were buying mascara, antacids, greeting cards, sunscreen. A man stood patiently comparing cough syrups. A woman scrolled her phone in line. The fluorescent lights hummed. The registers beeped.

Nothing had shifted.

My mother was dead.
One human being—the one who had anchored my beginning—was no longer on the planet.
And the candy aisle was fully stocked.

I moved slowly, trying to remember why I had come. I felt suspended a few inches outside myself, watching this version of me push a cart.

How is it possible, I wondered, that the machinery of the world continues untouched? That traffic lights change. That receipts print. That people make dinner plans.

How is it that the sun rises?
The world looked exactly the same.
I was the one who had changed.

Yesterday, I was someone whose mother was alive. Yesterday, I could time-travel backward simply by calling her. Yesterday, I was held in that quiet, invisible tether that exists between parent and child.

Today, that tether felt severed.
I am still me.
And I am not.
There is a particular loneliness in realizing that your internal
earthquake
registers as nothing
more than another Thursday
to everyone else. The world continues.

two

THE THING ABOUT GRIEF IS...

the world goes on

The thing about grief is that the world goes on looking the way it does. Normal things happen in the normal ways they always have.

We are changed.

surprised by the sun

The morning after the night my mother died, the sun came up.

You may be thinking, of course that happened.

And yet.

And yet, I was surprised when the sun came up.

I was surprised because I couldn't imagine that such a thing could happen,

seasonal

I wonder
if there's a season
that carries grief better than the others.

Both my parents died in winter.

You would think
the cold would keep it.

Fall lets go easily.
Leaves loosen their grip.
The garden thins to stem and husk.
Light slips away earlier each day.

Winter is not grief.
Winter is what remains.

Spring aches.
The first warm afternoon
with no one to call.
Daffodils opening
to an absence.

Summer is loud with green.
Heat pressing against the windows.
Children running through sprinklers.

An empty chair
at the edge of the pool.

Leaves fall.
Snow settles.
Crocuses push through.
The sun lingers.

Grief does not choose.

It sheds.
It freezes.
It blooms.
It burns.
It stays.

i should move on

I'm told I should move on from grief.
It's offered gently sometimes. Other times it lands like instruction. Like something I've forgotten to do.
I don't understand what "move on" even means.

Grief is not a highway shoulder I've pulled onto. It isn't a waiting room I've lingered in too long, flipping through outdated magazines. It is not a season I missed the memo about ending.

Move on to where?

Forward suggests there is a direction that doesn't include this. As if grief is a place behind me instead of something that rises with me each morning. As if it could be misplaced. Left at the curb. Donated. Outgrown.

But grief isn't behind me.

It is in the way my body still turns to say their names.
In the pause before I share good news.
In the way certain songs feel like they are happening to me instead of playing.

If I move, it moves.

It rides in the passenger seat. It stands beside me in the grocery line. It slips into bed at night and presses its quiet weight against my back.

Sometimes I think what they mean is: let it be smaller. Less visible. Less inconvenient.

But grief has its own gravity. It does not respond to willpower. It does not thin because I have been brave. It does not dissolve because enough time has passed.

It is not something I cling to.
It is something that matters.

There are losses that should not be stepped over.
There are names that should not fade.

I don't know how to move on from grief.
Some days it walks beside me.
Some days it drags its feet.
Some days it disappears just long enough for me to think maybe this is what they meant.
And then something small
a smell,
a name,
a light through a window,
and there it is.

Not behind me.
Not ahead.

Here.

And sometimes, in the middle of an ordinary afternoon,
I catch myself laughing.

For a moment
I forget to measure
where grief is standing.

I only notice
that I am still here.

practical

After someone dies, there are things to do.
Not metaphorical things. Not healing things.
Practical things.

You stand in a closet and look for clothes that meet three
requirements:
they fit,
you don't like them,
you will never wear them again.

You hold fabric between your fingers and think about
weather. About sleeves. About whether black is too
dramatic or not dramatic enough. As if this is a normal
decision. As if the world has not tilted on its axis.

You write a eulogy. You open a blank document and try
to summarize a life that built yours. You search for stories
that won't undo you in front of a room full of people
holding tissues.

You practice reading it out loud.
You drive to the funeral and to the cemetery.
You follow instructions. Park here. Stand there. Wait.

You watch the casket—the one that holds what is left of
your parent—hover for a moment above the open ground.

There are straps. There is choreography. There is a man who has done this before.

The casket lowers.
There is a sound when dirt hits a casket.
No one prepares you for that sound.

It is not cinematic. It is not soft. It is damp, cold mud mixed with rock. It lands with a dull insistence. Final without being loud.

You hear it once.
And then again.

Shovel
by
shovel.

Someone puts a hand on your back. Someone says something about closure. The sky continues doing whatever it was already doing.

And somewhere inside your chest, the comfortable knowing of how to be and who to be begins to loosen. The version of you that existed when they were alive fades at the edges. You feel it happening in real time—a quiet rearranging of streets you thought you knew by heart.

Still, the man with the shovel keeps working.

There are forms to sign. Cars to move. Flowers to gather.
Thank-you notes that will need to be written.
The world does not pause for the sound of dirt.

It just continues.

Shovel
by
shovel.

me in the after-grief

I'm in the after-grief.
Don't be confused—the after-grief doesn't mean grief is
over. It is not a finish line. It is a location.
Like the afterlife, only the after-grief is for the living.

It is where you wake up when the pastries and deli trays
are gone.
When the sympathy cards have been opened.
When the world has decided you are functional again.

Me in the after-grief carries a fear.
A deep-down fear that I will forget my parents.
Not all at once.
But slowly.

I will forget the warmth of their hands—
not the idea of it,
but the actual temperature.

I will forget the color of their eyes in certain light.
The way the color shifted when they were tired.
The way it sharpened when they laughed.

And I will forget the sound of their voices saying my name.

Not the fact that they said it.
But the way it landed.

If I forget what they sounded like when they spoke my
name,
who will know how I was meant to be called?

In the after-grief, I am afraid that forgetting is a second loss.
Quieter.
Less witnessed.

There is another fear here.
That I disappointed them.
That throughout our time together on this planet I did not
love well enough. Did not call enough. Did not understand
enough.
And now that they are gone, I fear I am still getting it wrong.
I don't visit them at the cemetery.
The truth is, I don't know what to do there.
The ground feels too literal. Too contained.

What if they expect me?
What if love requires geography?

In the after-grief, questions multiply.
They do not resolve.

They sit beside me at the kitchen table.
They ride home in the passenger seat.
They wait at the foot of the bed.

Grief is not over.
It is just less loud.
And sometimes that is what scares me most.

breathe in, breathe out

If you've ever had a lingering cough, you know the tickle.
It starts small.
A suggestion in the back of the throat.
A quiet clearing that doesn't quite clear.
I try to ignore it.

The tickle feels almost polite. It doesn't demand attention.
It waits. It reminds me it could become something louder
at any moment.

The bark is easier. It has edges.
I cough. It's loud. It's over.
There is relief in the clean beginning and end of it.

But the fit—
the one that arrives without asking—
is different.

It takes over.
It interrupts sentences.
It bends the body forward.
It steals breath and then asks for more.

There is never a good time for it.
I want it contained. Timed. Scheduled between obligations.

Instead, it rises.

Inconvenient.
Uncooperative.
Unimpressed by my plans.

Sometimes I try to swallow it.

Press it down.
Smooth my voice.
Sip water and pretend the body hasn't already decided.

But the more I hold it back,
the tighter my chest becomes.

The throat closes around what wants to move.
Even comfort can choke.
Even silence can press.

Grief is like that.

It begins as a tickle.
A memory at the wrong time.
A name spoken in passing.

If it barks, it comes and goes.
Sharp. Honest.

If it's swallowed,
it waits.

And sometimes it becomes a fit—
bending the body forward,
asking for air,
refusing to be polite.

There is no convenient time for grief.
There is only breath.
It rises.
It moves.
It takes the air it needs.

And afterward,
the chest loosens on its own.

Not because grief is gone.
Not because I have done anything right.
Just because the body cannot hold it forever.

witnessing

Must grief be witnessed?
I tell myself it does not.

I don't care if you are around to experience my pain or witness my grief.
I don't want or need your validation.
I do not need a nod, a hand on my back, a careful tone.

I especially do not need a sentence that begins with
"at least…"

At least they lived a long life.
At least they aren't suffering.
At least you had them as long as you did.
"At least" is a door closing quietly.

So I decide I do not need anyone to witness my grief.

My grief is intact without an audience.
It breathes whether you see it or not.
It wakes me in the night whether you understand it or not.

All parts of it are present—
the anger,
the tenderness,
the ache that sits behind the ribs—

even in your absence.

And still.

There are moments when the pain swells and I feel the
room tilt,
and I wonder what it would be like
if someone could stand inside it with me
without rearranging it.

Without fixing it.
Without shrinking it.
Without reaching for silver linings like bandages.

Not to witness as proof.
Not to validate.
Just to stay.

Because disappointment is heavy enough.
I do not need it added to the loss.

So I practice telling myself
I do not need anyone to see this.

And maybe that is partly strength.
And maybe it is also protection.
In the quiet, I can admit this much:
Grief does not require witnesses.
But sometimes my heart does.

they is me

They want us to move on.
They want us to be finished with grief.
They do not have time for the thick, heavy water of it.
 For the wading.
 For the circling back.
They want a road map.

Tell us where this leads.
Tell us how long it lasts.
Tell us when you will be yourself again.

They want us to stop wandering.
To stop wondering.
To laugh without the catch in our throat.
To be recognizable.

They want the version of us they knew before.
Sometimes they say it gently.
Sometimes not.

Get over it already.

I have called them impatient.
Unkind.
Unable to sit in the dark.

But mostly,
they are me.

I wanted to move on.
I wanted grief to behave.
To follow a timeline.
To thin out on schedule.

I wanted a road map.
A sign that said *you are here.*
An arrow pointing forward.

I wanted to stop wandering in my own life.
I wanted to recognize myself again.

I wanted to laugh and not feel disloyal.
I wanted to sleep and not dream in fragments.
I wanted the muddy water to clear so I could see my feet.

I wanted to get over it already.

I am the one who grew impatient.
The one who mistook endurance for failure.
The one who whispered, enough.

I am they.
And they are tired.

your parents would be so proud

I've heard it said many times,
"Your parents would be so proud of how you've handled
your grief."

I respond the way people respond.
Thank you.
The words come easily. They leave my mouth without
asking permission.

The world sees a daughter who has lost her parents and
keeps moving.
She smiles. She laughs. She hosts holidays. She dances
at her children's weddings. She tends to friendships. She
builds a life.

From the outside, it looks sturdy.
Beautiful, even.

And then someone tells me my parents would be proud.
And something in me recoils.

You don't know my parents.
You don't know what they would say.
You don't know the sound of their pride.

You don't know the weight of their silence.
You don't know the way they looked at the end.

When I hear that sentence, my mind does not go to pride.
It goes to the room in the house with the hospital bed.

To the sponge on a stick that moistens a mouth that can
no longer swallow.
To the spoons. The straws.
To the medications crushed into liquid because tablets
are no longer possible.
To the oxygen machine humming beside the bed.
To the mask. The tubing.
To the way "terminal restlessness" is a phrase that sounds
almost gentle until you see it.

I see mottled skin.
Dull eyes that once sparkled.
Hands I hold that once held me steady.
I see mouths open for air.
Chests rising and falling, slower each time.
Grey-blue skin.
Caskets.
A hole in the ground that feels too large for anything to
survive.

And someone tells me they would be proud.

Proud of what?

Of how I fold the napkins at Thanksgiving?
Of how I laugh without breaking in half?
Of how I manage to keep breathing?

My parents are not here to be proud.
They are not here to witness how I am doing this.
And I am not "handling" my grief.
I am living it.

Some days that looks like dancing.
Some days it looks like getting out of bed.
Some days it looks like nothing at all.

When you tell me they would be proud,
I nod.
Because I know what you mean.
But inside, I am still in that room.
Still holding their hands.
Still listening to machines breathe when they could not.
And there is nothing tidy or triumphant about that.

not so secret secrets

People stop checking in long before you stop needing them.

At first there are messages.
Thinking of you.
How are you holding up?

Then there is space.
If they think of you at all, they assume you've gotten better.
And in a way, you have.

You've gotten better at saying, "I'm okay."
Better at keeping your voice steady in the grocery store.
Better at not mentioning the hospital room that still lives in your mind.

Closure isn't something you can point to.
Silence is.

Not being able to call them is real.
Reaching for your phone and remembering is real.
The unsent sentences stacking up in your throat.

Grief isn't just crying.

It is crying.
It is also folding laundry.
Answering emails.
Standing in line with milk and bread and a heaviness no
one can see.

You aren't only grieving them.
You are grieving who you were when they were alive.
Joy feels different now.
Sometimes it arrives and you hesitate.
Sometimes you let yourself laugh and feel the sting of
guilt—
as if happiness has crossed a line.
You forget small things.
The exact scent of their shampoo.
The way their sweater smelled when you leaned in.
One day you will try to remember and come up empty.
That absence has weight.

in his element

My dad loved Costco.
He and his friends would talk for hours about Costco.
They loved to describe things like the "fall off the bone
leg of lamb" in the same sentence with the "cushy 12 pairs
of mid-calf tube socks" that elevated their New Balance
running shoes.
Nobody ran.

When my mom was no longer able to walk the aisles (and
aisles) of stuff at Costco, I became Dad's shopping partner.
Dad always promised I could "get stuff too."
As I look back on it, a trip to Costco was one of the ways
my dad was saying he was lonely, bored, and looking to
fill the emptiness. And at the same time he was telling
me that he wanted to spend time with me.

He wanted to spend time with me.

I railed against the invitation too consumed by my disdain
for the bright lights, the blowing air and the crowds. I was
dug in too deep with my ick for gigantic carts filled with
items that did not belong together like pillows, shoes,
salmon, 24 eggs, beef tenderloin, adult "underwear" and
danish large enough to feed a small country.

After my mom died, and shortly before Dad's death, I set my shit aside and we went to Costco. South Florida Costco. If you know, you know. If you don't, imagine aggressive shoppers, lots of lines, and even more air conditioning. Frozen-tundra level air conditioning.

The trip was memorable for several reasons not limited to Dad being in a wheelchair, hood up to fight the conditioned air tundra, and forgetting his eyeglasses, which led to sunglasses indoors. There was something slightly pathetic about the sight of Dad, and at the same time it was kind of hilarious. He had serious range that day, looking like he needed all the help in the world, but showing up like a Unibomber mob boss. Dad ordered me about (in the best way possible) filling the cart with gusto.

Being a true Costco super-fan, Dad was in his element that day.
On our way home from Costco, we strategized a dinner menu made from our big shop.
The moment felt magical.
Perfect.
Normal.

Two days later, Dad had a heart attack.
The beginning of the end for Dad.
I kept his feet warm, covering them in cushy tube socks.
Nobody ran.

lately i'm late

Time is the thing that gets in the way.
Start times do not consider grief.
Calendars do not soften.

There are invitations.
There are expectations.
There are doors that open at seven.

Before I walk in, I am in the car longer than necessary.
Before I get into bed, I scroll back through old texts,
reading the ordinary words
as if they might rearrange themselves
into something living.

Before I come to dinner,
before I show up anywhere,
there is a negotiation.

Stay home.
Cancel.
Disappear into pajamas and the dim light of the television.
Let the world continue without me.

Grief stretches time in one direction
and the clock pulls it in another.

Five minutes can hold a year.
A whole evening can pass without me ever arriving inside it.

I am often late.
Not because I don't care.

But because I am standing in the hallway of my own life,
trying to gather myself
from rooms that no longer exist.

For what feels like the thousandth time,
I say I'm sorry.

And what I mean is—
I am still learning how to arrive.

earned

I do not know what it means to "heal" from grief.
Heal into what?
A life where their names do not alter the air.
A morning that does not begin with the fact of them missing.

People speak of healing as if grief were an injury.
As if it should close.
But this is not something that closes.
It is something that remains.

There were years before this.
Years of ordinary acts—
rides to the airport,
holidays argued over and hosted,
dishes dried and put away,
voices calling my name from another room.
All of that does not disappear simply because they did.

I earned this grief.
Not through tragedy.
Through time.
Through repetition.
Through showing up when it was inconvenient.
Through staying when it was easier not to.
Grief is what is left in the body after that kind of living.

It is muscle memory.
It is reflex.
It is the space their absence carves and refuses to refill.

I will not hurry it.
I will not measure it against someone else's timeline.

If it thins, it will thin on its own.
If it shifts, it will do so without my permission.

But I will not treat it like an illness to recover from.
It is proof that something real stood here.
And I am not ready to pretend otherwise.

three

THE THING ABOUT GRIEF IS...

it's precious

You don't have to take on my grief. I didn't ask you to. You can't process my grief for me. Only I can do that. It's mine.

sharing messages

My dad acknowledges my presence with his eyebrows.
A lift.
A squint of eyes that have spent more time closed than open.
It is the smallest movement,
and it feels enormous.

I sit beside him and read messages from his friends.

Men who have known him longer than I have been alive.
Men who use words like loyal. Steady. Generous.
Men who remember stories I have never heard.
Their sentences are thick with history.
I read them out loud.

My voice catches on certain phrases—
"the kind of man you could count on,"
"the one who showed up,"
"the way he held us together."

It takes nearly everything in me not to unravel.

The room is quiet except for the hum of air moving through machines.
Except for my own breathing, trying to stay even.
Except for the weight of what is leaving.

I want him to hear who he has been.
I want him to know that the life he built reached further
than this bed.

There is something almost unbearable
about learning your parent in reverse—
through the mouths of others,
at the edge of goodbye.

And still, I keep reading.
Because there is a gift in it.

In hearing the shape of him reflected back.
In knowing he did not simply pass through this world
unnoticed.
He pressed into it.
He altered it.

My dad lifts his eyebrows again.
A flicker.
And I understand that this, too, is precious.

every dream begins with a dreamer

Dad is comfortable, peaceful, mostly unable to respond.

He looks like someone who is sleeping deeply.
Crisp sheets.
Pristine cotton blankets.
An 800-thread-count pillowcase on a perfectly fluffed
pillow—not overly fluffed, because, Dad—
resting on a real mattress we chose instead of the thin
hospital one.

Even now, we want him comfortable.
I sit beside him and wonder what he is dreaming.
And then I wonder if a body softened by methadone and
morphine even reaches dreams at all.
Hopeful me decides it does.
I hope he is dreaming of the times he was most himself.

The days he said, "fuck it, I'm out," and left work when
we were sick.
The way he showed up at school productions and games,
arms crossed, pretending not to care, caring entirely.
The magazines he'd toss onto my bed—Tiger Beat, Mad,
Good & Plenty tucked into the fold—
as if sugar and glossy paper could fix everything.

I hope he is dreaming of airports and maps spread across
kitchen tables.
Of walking beside Mom in cities that felt bigger than fear.
Of choosing adventure when staying small would have
been easier.

I hope he is dreaming of the moments he grew quiet
before speaking truth.
The times he let himself be known.
That was his bravest shape.

And I hope—selfishly—
that somewhere in the dream he is laughing.

The loud, ricocheting, ceiling-shaking HAAAAA-HAAAAA
that startled small children and dogs
and filled every room it entered.

If he is dreaming,
I hope he feels the warmth of the life he made.

Not perfect.
Not always easy.

But chosen.
Conscious.
His.
He lies there, still.
And I sit beside him,
holding all of it for him now.
Sweet dreams, Dad.

stay

Grief is not a beast.
It does not chase me.
It stays.

It waits in rooms that used to hold your body.
It rests on the pillow beside mine.
It lingers in the air like warmth that has nowhere to land.

Sometimes it presses against my chest.
Sometimes it walks beside me quietly.

It lets me laugh.
It does not always interrupt.
But it never leaves.
They say time heals all wounds.
Time does not heal this.
Time simply teaches me how to carry grief without dropping it in public.

Grief is not a moment.
It is not an event.

It is woven in.
It moves when I move.
It sits down when I sit down.

It reminds me that I once stood in the light of something
extraordinary.
And I hold it close.

Not because I enjoy the ache.
Not because I mistake pain for devotion.

But because within this ache is the outline of you.

To loosen my grip on grief
would feel like letting you disappear
again.

love is alive

It feels wrong to say this out loud.
But I love my grief.
I don't want to let it go.

No one is asking me to.
No one is standing over me with a timeline.

And still, I hold it carefully.

Like something breakable.
Like something that could be misplaced.

Oh.
It is precious.

Not because it feels good.
Not because it is noble.
But because it is what remains when the ordinary ways
of loving are gone.

I can no longer bring my dad the newspaper on Sunday
mornings.
I can no longer call my mom just to say I'm on my way
home.
I can no longer do the small, invisible things that used to
carry love back and forth between us.

Those gestures have nowhere to go.
But the love itself did not disappear.
It did not follow them into the ground.
It stayed.

It stayed in my chest.
In my hands.
In the reflex to reach for a phone that will not ring the
same way again.

My parents are dead.
My love is not.
It lives here now.
It moves through me with nowhere else to land.

That movement—
that ache—that constant turning toward what is no longer
there—
that is grief.

I do not want to let it go.
Because to let it go would feel like asking my love to
leave, too.
And I have already said goodbye once.

holding sadness close

Am I too comfortable with sadness?
I ask myself that sometimes.

The world around me insists that happiness is the goal.
Before grief, I believed that too.

I made happiness a priority.
Not because I understood it,
but because I thought I was supposed to.

I chased light without knowing what it illuminated.
Grief rearranged that.

After loss, sadness did not feel like failure.
It felt honest.

It had weight.
History.
A reason.

My sadness is not decorative.
It is not dramatic.

It carries time in it—
roles reversed,

hands held in hospital rooms,
voices that no longer answer.

There is nothing glamorous about it.
And yet I do not rush it away.

Sometimes that makes me wonder
if I have made sadness into something sacred.

If I am holding it too tightly.
But this sadness is not a mood.

It is the shape love took
once it could no longer move outward.

It lives in my eyes—
in the way I linger when someone is speaking.
In the way my chest tightens without warning.

It teaches me what mattered
by what still aches.

It reminds me where love once stood
by the space it refuses to surrender.

Happiness used to be a goal.
Now honesty is.
And some days, honesty looks like sadness.

living alongside absence

Grief does not announce itself as a teacher.
It stays.

It returns on days I thought were ordinary.
It settles somewhere behind the ribs
until the body adjusts around it.

I notice it in small ways.

In the way my eyes linger a little longer
when someone mentions a father,
a mother,
hospice.

In the pause before my heart opens fully again.

There is a new instinct now—
a quiet recognition
that something fragile is always at work beneath the
surface.

Time feels different.

A dinner stretches.
A goodbye lasts a beat longer than it used to.

A hand held across a table carries more weight than it
once did.

Nothing looks dramatic from the outside.
And yet everything feels slightly altered.
I did not set out to learn this.
Loss made the adjustments for me.

Now when I love,
I feel the edges of it.

Not fear.
Not hesitation.

Just the knowing
that nothing living stays untouched.

Absence moves in beside presence.
They do not cancel each other out.

They share the room.

And somehow,
the heart makes space for both.

why we stay

Sometimes I notice the moment when the ache loosens.
It happens without ceremony.

A full breath.
A laugh that comes too easily.
An afternoon that passes without their name brushing
against it.

And something in me stiffens.
As if I have stepped too far from them.
As if relief is disloyal.

There is a quiet fear in that softening—
that if the pain thins,
so will they.

Grief has been the place where I still feel closest.

Not in the sharpest days.
Not in the unraveling.

But in the steady ache that keeps them near the surface.

When it eases, even briefly,
I wonder who I am without it.

The world calls that healing.

I am not always sure.

Because grief has been a room I can enter
and find them waiting in memory.

The chair they used to sit in.
The sound of their laugh caught in the ceiling.
The shape of their absence, familiar as furniture.

To leave that room—even for a moment—
can feel like closing a door twice.

And yet I do leave.

I step into days that are lighter.
I breathe without measuring the air.

They do not vanish.

But the closeness shifts.

And I am still learning
how to love them
without clutching the ache that proves they were here.

i wait

Days keep their shape.
Morning. Coffee. Email. Evening.
And yet something inside me does not move with them.
Time passes. The calendar flips. Seasons change their light.

But the fact of it—
that they are gone—
does not loosen.

I thought grief would be louder.
Instead, it is a kind of stillness.
Not peace.

Just the same ache,
arriving each morning as if nothing has been processed
overnight.

I wait for something to shift.

For the first day I wake and do not feel it immediately.
For a memory to arrive without rearranging the air in the
room.

But most days, the feeling is unchanged.

It sits in the same place.
Not dramatic.

Not sharp.

Just there.
The sameness unsettles me.

I move through whole weeks and cannot point to any
difference.
I wonder if I am missing a milestone.
If grief is something other people graduate from.

From the outside, I look fine.

I answer.
I attend.
I participate.

Inside, I am still standing in the moment I understood
they were gone.
The world keeps layering new days on top of that one.

I wait—
not for grief to disappear,
but for the disbelief to soften.

For the ordinary to feel ordinary again.
Sometimes I think the waiting is the grief.

Not dramatic.
Not cinematic.

Just the quiet repetition of knowing

and knowing again
and knowing again
that this is true.

And still, I stay with it.

Not because I am noble.
Not because I am afraid to move.

But because love does not hurry its own undoing.

i feel like staying

The first time I said it out loud, my voice shook.
Not the whole story.
Just a sentence.

"My parents are dead."

The words felt too large for the room.
I expected them to fracture something.

Instead, there was a pause.

Not awkward.
Not pitying.

Just space.

I had been carrying that sentence carefully,
as if speaking it would expose me,
as if grief were something to tuck in,
to manage quietly.

When I said it, I noticed something shift.
Not in them.
In me.

My shoulders dropped a fraction.
The air reached further into my lungs.

I hadn't realized how tightly I was holding it.

There are days I still edit myself.

I soften the edges.
I say "I'm fine."
I keep the details small so the room stays comfortable.

But sometimes I let the truth land where it will.

"I miss them."
"This is still hard."
"I didn't expect it to feel like this."

The words don't fix anything.
They don't make the loss smaller.
But they make it less hidden.

And when it is less hidden,
I feel less alone inside it.

Sometimes someone nods.
Sometimes someone says, "Me too."
Sometimes nothing happens at all.

But even then, I know I have not erased what mattered.

I am still here.
It still happened.

And the saying of it—

even quietly—
feels like staying.

good grief

My parents are dead.
Even now, writing that feels abrupt.
Too clean for what it holds.

It has been more than three years since my mom died.
Ten months after that, my dad followed.

Time has passed.
But the way I live with their absence does not look like time.
It looks like a scribble across a page.
Not a line.
Not a sequence.
A scribble.

If you remember the Peanuts cartoons, you know Pigpen—
the small boy who walks through the world with a cloud
of dust following him.

That's what these years have felt like.
A dust cloud that never fully settles.

From the outside, it might look like dirt.
Like something unkempt.
Unresolved.

Inside it, though, is everything.

Sadness that arrives without warning.
Laughter that feels almost disloyal.
Longing that presses against my ribs.
Moments of steadiness that surprise me.

There are days I feel buried.
There are days I feel almost clear.

People talk about stages.
I have not found them.

I have found overlap.
Contradiction.
Joy and anger sharing the same hour.
Relief and guilt breathing side by side.

From a distance, it might look chaotic.

But inside the dust cloud is love.

Not tidy.
Not linear.
Just human.

I am still walking through it.
Still followed by it.

And maybe that is what grief looks like after both your
parents are gone—
not a path forward,

but a life carried inside a moving cloud
that proves something real once stood here.

reliable

I find myself bringing them up.
In small ways.

A story about something my dad once said.
The way my mom used to fold napkins.
A sentence that begins with, "They would have loved this."

Sometimes I notice I am the one who says their names first.
Out loud.

Not dramatically.
Just enough so they stay in the room.

There are days I tell the stories easily.
There are days my voice catches halfway through and I
have to decide whether to keep going.

I keep going.

Not because I am strong.
Not because I am trying to prove anything.
It just feels wrong to let their names sit untouched.

The rituals come back to me without effort.
The holidays they shaped.
The phrases they repeated.
The small habits that outlived them.

I hold onto some of it.
I let some of it change.

When I laugh and then feel tears at the edge of it, I don't
correct myself anymore.
Both can be true.
I don't think of this as legacy.
It feels more ordinary than that.
It feels like love continuing to move through the only body
it has left to move through.
So I say their names.
Again.
Not loudly.
Just enough.

witnessing grief while grieving

Grief pulls my attention inward, toward the place where loss lives in the body. Even when I am among others, I move as if underwater, aware of everything and yet wanting nothing to touch me. I did not imagine myself as someone who would ever invite grief in, let alone stand beside others as they entered their own.

At the site, I made slow and quiet moves to end our time there. I didn't want to speak to anyone. I didn't want to meet their gaze. Grief had already taken up all the space I could manage. The presence of other people's sorrow felt too close, too exposed, as if one wrong look might split something open I was still holding together.

The sun was warm that day. I remember how it settled on my skin, almost insistently, warming the cold I felt inside. The contrast was jarring—the body receiving comfort while the heart remained unreachable. Even now, that warmth feels like a question I did not know how to answer.

To witness grief while grieving is a particular kind of weight. It asks for attention when there is very little left to give. It asks you to stay open when your instinct is to protect what remains intact. I felt myself bracing against other people's pain, not out of indifference, but because I recognized it too well. Their loss echoed my own, and the echo was exhausting.

I used to believe grief was something private, something to be endured quietly and alone. Standing there, surrounded by others carrying their own unbearable truths, I realized how fragile that belief was. Grief does not arrive one at a time. It gathers. It overlaps. It moves through rooms and bodies without regard for our readiness.

What surprised me was not how much it hurt to witness, but how much it asked of me simply to remain present. I was not there to fix anything or to offer language. I was there to stand inside the shared silence, to let grief exist without being managed. That kind of witnessing felt like exposure, like allowing myself to be seen at a moment when I wanted nothing more than to disappear.

And yet, something steady lived inside that moment. Not comfort, not relief—something quieter. A recognition that grief does not only isolate; it also reveals. To witness another's sorrow while carrying your own is to understand how little distance there truly is between us. How thin the boundary is between my pain and yours.

I did not leave that place lighter. But I left altered. A little less certain that grief must always be faced alone. A little more aware that even in my own breaking, I am capable of staying. That I can stand in the warmth of the sun, feel the cold inside me, and bear both at once—my grief, and the presence of another's.

hear more /
here more

In grief, absence has a sound.
Not the hush I expected,
but something clearer—
as if the world has lowered its voice
and left yours intact.

When you were here,
life pressed in from all sides.
Your words lived among errands, weather,
the small negotiations of ordinary days.
I heard you, yes—
but I did not always *listen*.
Presence is busy.
It assumes time.

Now there is only the space you left,
and it is exact.
Your cadence still moves through it.
The pause before you answered.
The tone you used when you were certain,
and when you were trying to be kind.

I do not summon you.
You arrive.

In the quiet grief makes,
your voice finds me
without effort.

It feels dangerous to admit this—
as if clarity now
means failure then.
But grief is not a verdict.
It is a narrowing.
Everything unnecessary falls away,
and what remains speaks.

You live in the way I decide,
in the words I reach for
when I am tired or afraid.
Loss did not create this.
It revealed it.
Grief slowed my breathing
until I could hear
what was already inside me.

This does not comfort me.
It sharpens the ache.
To hear you so clearly
is to know exactly what is gone.

You are not here.
I do not pretend otherwise.
But in the space where breath catches,

where the world holds still for a moment,
I hear you—
and I carry that sound forward,
not to replace you,
but to remember how love once breathed
between us.

four

THE THING ABOUT GRIEF IS...

it's a silent watcher

Grief is your constant companion once you welcome it into your life *(or even if you don't)*.

footsteps

Turning around to walk away from you was excruciatingly difficult. Painful as if my body was made of stiff, unbending wire. My back to you felt like an insult.

I turned my head toward you for one more look, hoping this one would capture everything about you that I didn't want to forget.

You were gone.

Your soul had left the room.

And I couldn't imagine leaving you.

I wanted to stay.

I wanted to say whatever hadn't been said.

I wanted you and I to be complete.

I wanted to tell you I wasn't ready and if I could, I would undo your death.

I wanted to stay.

Nobody prepares you for leaving.

Nobody mentions that in the end, leaving is all that's left.

Nobody guides you in the ways of walking while resisting walking.

So final.

I don't know if anyone ever gets over that walk.

I haven't.

Not yet.

I have it on replay most days, an endless loop.
The silence.
The smell.
The darkness.
The sound of getting up, turning away from you.

enough for now

I didn't arrive at self-compassion because I was wise.
I arrived because everything else had failed.

Grief made me clumsy with myself. I forgot to eat. I stayed too long. I apologized for breathing. I learned how quickly I could turn absence into accusation—how easily I could believe that if I were better, quieter, stronger, this wouldn't hurt so much.

Self-compassion sounded suspicious then. Like something for people who were already healed. People with clean kitchens and calendars that made sense. People who hadn't learned to brace their bodies against the day.

What I knew how to do was endure.

Grief sharpened my inner voice. It kept a tally. You should be further along by now. You shouldn't still feel this way. Other people are managing. I carried those sentences like stones in my pockets, proof that I was failing something unnamed but important.

And yet—there were moments I couldn't keep up the punishment.
Moments when the weight of it made me sit down on the floor.

Those moments weren't gentle. They weren't pretty. They were pauses forced by exhaustion. But in them, something loosened. I noticed how hard I had been gripping myself. How grief had turned me into both the wounded and the one doing the wounding.

Self-compassion didn't arrive as forgiveness.
It arrived as a ceasefire.

Even then, it felt dangerous. Like desertion. Like if I stopped hurting myself on purpose, I might be abandoning the one I had lost. As if vigilance were a form of love. As if pain were the only proof that I was still paying attention.

Kindness felt like betrayal before it felt like relief.

It sounded like: enough for now.
It looked like staying in bed without narrating it as a moral failure.
It felt like letting tears come without asking them to justify themselves.

I didn't trust it. Softening felt like turning my back. Like leaving the house with the lights off, unsure if I'd be forgiven for not keeping watch. I worried that if I grew gentler, grief would slip away—and I would lose them all over again.

But grief had already taken so much. I was tired of helping it.

Choosing self-compassion didn't mean I suddenly liked myself. It meant I stopped interrogating every instinct. It meant letting grief be messy without making that mess a verdict on my character.

Most days, self-compassion was not a choice I made once. It was a choice I forgot and remembered again. I would catch myself mid-spiral—halfway through a familiar rehearsal of blame—and feel a small, quiet resistance. Not confidence. Just fatigue with cruelty.

We aren't good at this. We are trained to be useful, resilient, and improved. We know how to push. We don't know how to stay.

Self-compassion asks us to stay with what is tender without trying to earn relief. That feels unnatural. Like learning a language without verbs. Like holding a crying child and realizing the child is you.

Some days, I still reach for harshness out of habit. It's familiar. It feels loyal. It feels like keeping faith. But it leaves me lonelier than grief ever did.

So when I can, I choose something smaller.

I choose not to correct my sadness.
I choose to believe that my nervous system is doing its best with a shattered map.
I choose to sit beside myself instead of standing over.

This is not healing as transformation.
It is healing as accompaniment.

And on the days I manage it—even briefly—I notice something surprising: grief does not grow larger when I am kind to myself. It grows quieter. It breathes. It becomes something I can carry instead of something that carries me.

I am still learning. Still awkward. Still forgetting.

But sometimes, in the middle of an ordinary, undone day, I feel my body unclench just enough to rest its weight. And in that small mercy, I understand that self-compassion is not a betrayal after all.

It is how I keep love with me—without bleeding myself dry.

at the same table

Both of my sons were married within a short span of time.
Not long after the death of each of my parents.

The seasons overlapped.
White dresses and dark clothes hung in the same closet.
Vows were practiced in rooms where grief still echoed.

At the weddings, my parents were not in the front row.
Their chairs stayed empty,
polite, unmistakable.
I kept noticing them the way you notice a missing tooth—
your tongue returning again and again
to the space where something once lived.

I missed my mother in the small, unnecessary moments—
the way she would have sparkled in sensible but expensive
shoes,
the way she would have pressed her hand to her chest
as if love required containment.
I missed my father in the noisy parts,
in the loud and raucous parts that would have sat beside
me, bigger than life and solid as stone.

And still—
joy kept finding me.

It moved through the room like music you don't realize
has already entered your body.
It lived in my sons' faces—
how steady they looked,
how open.
It shimmered in the light on glass,
in the gathered breath before *I do*,
in the way love seemed to rise and stand on its own two
feet.

I felt grief at the same time.
Dense.
A low tide pulling at my ribs.

For a moment I wondered if joy was allowed.
If welcoming it would mean leaving my parents behind.
If smiling would loosen my grip on what I had already lost.

But grief did not ask me to be alone.

So I let joy sit with us.
Right there at the table.
Grief took one chair—
familiar, weighty, honest.
Joy took another—
warm, a little unsure,
hands folded in its lap.

They did not speak to each other.
They didn't need to.

They shared the same candlelight,
the same clinking glasses,
the same breath moving in and out of my chest.

I cried during the vows.
I laughed at the toasts. I danced without abandon. My
hands shook.
My heart stayed open.

I carried my parents with me that day—
in absence,
in memory,
in love that had nowhere to go but deeper inside.

And I let something else stay too.
A living joy.
Not instead of grief,
but alongside it.

Two truths.
One table.
My heart wide enough
to hold what ended
and what had just begun.

breaking hearts
have no sound

People ask what a breaking heart sounds like.
They expect shattering. Glass. A clean, cinematic noise
that announces itself.

But heartbreak is quieter than that.

If there is a sound, it isn't sudden. It doesn't explode.
It thins.

It is the sound of a room after someone leaves, and the
air hasn't learned how to move yet.
The low hum of the refrigerator at three in the morning,
suddenly loud because there is nothing else to hold the
space.
The pause before your name when someone asks how
you are.

A breaking heart sounds like breath forgetting its rhythm.
Like the extra second before an inhale decides to come
back.

Sometimes it sounds like your body doing ordinary
things—washing a mug, tying a shoe—while something
inside you refuses to cooperate. A small lag. A delay. The

sense that your hands are ahead of you and your heart
is still elsewhere.

If there is a crack, it's not jagged.
It's dulled.

It sounds like words losing their edges.
Like laughter that arrives late and leaves early.
Like music you've heard a thousand times, suddenly
failing to reach you.

A breaking heart sounds like restraint.
Like holding back tears not because you are strong, but
because you are tired.
Like swallowing sentences you used to say without
thinking.

It can sound like nothing at all.

That's the most confusing part—the way grief can be silent
and still be screaming. The way absence has weight but
no volume. You listen for proof and hear only your own
pulse, suddenly louder, suddenly unreliable.

Sometimes the sound is internal:
a soft, repetitive thud—hope knocking and being turned
away.
Sometimes it's the sound of your thoughts circling the
same memory, the same moment, wearing a groove into
the day.

A breaking heart doesn't announce itself.
It infiltrates.

It sounds like staying very still so you don't make it worse.
Like choosing quiet because noise might split you open
the rest of the way.

And yet—if you listen long enough—there is another sound
beneath it. Faint. Uneven. Not comforting, exactly, but
alive.

The sound of a heart still working, even damaged.
Still pumping love through a body that doesn't know
where to put it.
Still insisting, softly, on continuation.

A breaking heart does not shatter.
It changes its acoustics.

It learns how to hold sorrow without letting it echo too far.
It learns how to beat without applause.
It learns how to make room for silence and survive it.

That, I think, is the sound.

Not the break itself—but what remains afterward.

a voice

Grief is a voice that needs to speak.

Sometimes it whispers—
an inside voice, thin enough to pass as my own.
Sometimes it rises without warning.
Sometimes it shouts.

In my experience, it grows louder
when it hasn't been spoken to.

It doesn't wait for permission.
It doesn't follow the rules of conversation.
It interrupts.
It lingers.
It hums beneath everything—
a low electrical current I carry with me.

I don't know if others hear it.
But I do.

I hear it in my ears.
I see it in my eyes.
I feel it moving through my body,
settling where words usually live.

I've learned that when I don't acknowledge it,

when I pretend not to hear,
the voice sharpens.
Edges form.

Late at night, it becomes clearest.

I don't know why this hour belongs to the voice of grief.
Only that when the house goes still,
when the world loosens its grip,
the voice finds me.

Lying in bed,
in the dark,
with nothing left to distract me,
I feel it arrive.

And if I stay still enough,
if I don't rush to quiet it
or turn away,
the voice softens.

It doesn't disappear.
It doesn't leave.

It waits—
listening with me
for what comes next...

everywhere and nowhere

Losing someone doesn't happen once.
It happens again and again—
in the ordinary moments that forget to warn you.
You see something: a movie they loved, a sunset they would have stopped to name.
Your body leans toward the familiar thought—*I should tell them about this*—
and for a breath, it feels possible.
Then the truth returns.
Not loudly. Not dramatically.
Just the steady fact of it: they are not coming back. They are never coming back.
You sit with the ache as if it's new, even though you've met it before.
It pins you in place.
It asks nothing.
It takes everything.
And still, you live.
You move, putting one foot in front of the other.
You laugh again, surprised by the sound of your own voice.
But some part of you stays alert, listening.
Waiting for a door to open.
Waiting for footsteps that belong to a life you loved.

Maybe that's what grief is—
loving someone who has no fixed address anymore,
who lives everywhere and nowhere all at once.

how would you love me through this?

If I imagine you speaking, imagine you loving me through this, you would tell me...

You are who I wanted to be.
You are who I would not let myself be.
You are who I thought I would be, planned to be.

You are who I needed as a role model.
You are who I turned away from because the truth of who you are, who you could not help yourself from being, reflected the contentment-lie that I lived.

You are freedom.
I was never free on that side of the door.
I am free now on this side
I see myself in you.

That feels strange and also aspirational and also intimidating.
And over here I get to be without rules.

You need you.
Keep listening. Trusting. Making it up.

Your family needs you.

Know the difference between connection and neediness.

The world needs you.
You know that. It's OK to know that and respond.
It's OK to love that greatness inferno that happens when you respond.
Don't hold back for fear of burning down the house.

in my dreams

They come to me in my dreams.

Not together.
Not often.
But clearly.

Sometimes it's my mother. Sometimes my father. Sometimes I don't realize who they are until the dream is already ending, the way you don't notice the light until it's gone.

In my dreams, they are not sick.
They are not dying.
They are not already gone.

They are just there.

My mother appears close to me, the way she always did—near enough that I can feel her presence without her touching me. Her voice is right. Her timing is perfect. She says something sharp or brilliant or unexpectedly gentle, and I feel that familiar click of recognition. Of course. Of course she would say that.

My father shows up differently.

He is confident.

Busy.
Fully himself.

He moves through the dream the way he moved through
life—going about his business, offering advice, telling
people exactly what they need to hear whether they want
to hear it or not. He makes himself central. Useful.

In my dreams I tell him he is dead.

When I wake up, the happiness comes first.
A warmth in my chest.
A quiet thrill.

They were there, I think.
I saw them.

For a few moments, I carry the feeling that the connection
still exists—that love has found a way around death.

Then the sadness arrives.

Not dramatically.
Just faithfully.

I remember that the conversation is over.
That I can't return.
That the only place they come back to me is in my sleep.

I am grateful for these dreams.
And I am undone by them.

They give me my parents back just long enough to remind
me what it felt like to be known, corrected, loved.

And then I wake up—
happy that I found them,
sad that it was only a dream.

returning to the window

Floor to ceiling, three hurricane-proof glass sliding doors overlooked the green-blue beauty of the Gulf of Mexico. Through them, I felt the warm, sunny breeze of a typical day in the Florida Keys. It smelled good—familiar, even.

What felt even more familiar, though, was what lived inside.

Just beyond those doors, inside the house, was a hospital bed. It appeared back in February, shortly after I heard the words *no more interventions, comfort measures only* come out of my mouth.

I spent hours each day looking through those doors as my mother inched her way out of this world and into the next.

Just under ten months later, the focus shifted to my eighty-eight-year-old dad. I heard myself echo that same sentence again: *no more interventions, comfort measures only.*

It was easy enough to write. Much harder to say. And devastating in the moments that followed.

The hospital bed returned to its place by the floor-to-ceiling, hurricane-proof sliding doors overlooking the Gulf of Mexico.

muted but present

Most hotel rooms have the same kind of curtain—the flimsy one that hangs just inside the heavier drapes. Not meant to block anything, really. Not light, not sound, not the world. It's more of a suggestion than a barrier.

Grief feels like that.

A thin, sheer layer between me and everything else.

Light passes through it. LIfe continues on the other side. I can see shapes moving—people laughing in the parking lot, cars pulling in and out, morning arriving whether I am ready or not. Nothing is fully hidden. Nothing is fully clear.

When I wake in grief, the world is filtered. Muted but present. Softened and distorted at the same time. I am still here, still in the room, still breathing—but there is always something between me and what I'm looking at.

I can reach out and touch the curtain. I can pull it back for a moment—step into conversation, into laughter, into ordinary life. But it never stays open for long. It drifts back into place, light and persistent, reminding me that something has changed.

The curtain doesn't stop the sun. It doesn't stop the day from happening. It only alters how it arrives.

That's what grief does. It lets life in, but not all at once. It diffuses joy. It softens pain. It makes everything seem slightly out of focus, as if I'm always looking through something thin and tender and easily torn.

Some days I resent the curtain. I want clear glass. I want nothing between me and the world. Other days I am grateful for its mercy—for the way it filters what would otherwise be too bright, too sharp, too much.

Grief is not the heavy drape we pull shut. It is the sheer one we live behind.

Always moving. Never fully open. Never fully closed.

the view from below

"They" say grief comes in waves.
I don't know who "they" are, but I agree.

For me, grief came as a pool.
A pool painted blue, black lane lines stretching along
the bottom,
surrounded by a cement deck.

When I imagine my grief, I see myself underwater.
The water is tolerable—meant to be refreshing.
But it isn't.
It's too cold.

I am swimming.
Heading for the shallow end.
Ready to come up.

From below, I can see people on the pool deck.
Their bodies blur and bend, faces distorted by the surface.
I hear them, but only faintly—
muffled by water and distance.

Mostly, I hear my own heartbeat.
Rhythmic. Heavy.
For a moment, I'm comforted by its familiarity.

I know this sound.
It has been with me as long as I have been alive.

I am ready for air.

That's the thing.
I can't break the surface.

I can see it—
right there, beneath the distorted figures above me.
So close.

I can't reach them.
They don't notice.

I've always been a strong swimmer.
The people on the deck know this.
They trust me to stay afloat.

They don't look my way.
They don't worry.

I'm not panicking.
I'm frustrated.

I need help.
I need someone to see me.

They don't.

It is up to me to break the surface.

It is up to me to breathe.
It is up to me to keep living.

my mother's arms

I don't know that I will ever be over grief.
I don't know how you get over something that is both whole and shapeless at the same time.
Grief isn't loud most days.
It slips in.

I remember a warm, bright afternoon in late fall.
One of those rare Cleveland days that arrives after you've already accepted winter.
The sun warmed my sad, cold bones.

I breezed into CVS, lighthearted, full Katrina and the Waves, walking on sunshine, on a simple mission for toothpaste.
Mint. Fluoride.
Nothing in my head but the small satisfaction of good dental hygiene.
Grief stayed outside.

Then there she was.

Slowly emerging from the chaos barely contained in aisle 14—Analgesics.
She leaned into a red CVS shopping cart, using it to steady herself.
Her sleeveless arms gripped the handle.

Those arms.

I didn't know her.
But I knew those arms.

My mother's arms.
Spotted by sun and years.
Upper arms softened into crepey skin, folded and slack
in a way that only time allows.

I know those arms.
Or maybe I know what they remind me of.
The arms I knew didn't always look like that.

For a moment, I wasn't sure where I was.
CVS wavered.
Time thinned.
I stood between toothpaste and memory, watching a
stranger wear my mother's body.

I imagine—because imagination is all I have—what it felt
like to be held by those arms when they were tighter,
more vital.

Broken in by my siblings before me.
Strong from carrying children, groceries, the ordinary
weight of a life.

Those arms exist now only in my mind.
I don't fully trust the memory.

Grief edits as much as it preserves.

What I hold instead are the arms of age.
Of wisdom earned and paid for.
Of existing, withering, shrinking, becoming brittle.

These are the arms of my mother that live in my heart.

Warm.
Calm.
Wrapped.
Secure.

And still—

Standing there in CVS, I felt the distance between what
I remember and what I can reach.
How even love thins with time.
How memory keeps changing its shape.

I picked up my toothpaste.
I paid.
I walked back out into the sunlight.

And grief, unfinished and uninvited,
came with me.

ordinary days

If you're anything like me, you thought the hardest day after losing someone would be the day of the funeral.
If you've lost someone very close to you, you likely know now that the grief on that day—while heavy—is not the worst of it.
Not that day.
Not even their birthday.

In the months leading up to the one-year mark of my mother's death, I believed that day would undo me.
I braced myself for it.
I counted toward it.
I survived it.

In my experience, the hardest day is the one that arrives without warning.
Uneventful.
Ordinary.

It's the kind of day where nothing is marked on the calendar.
The kind of day when joy or beauty or humor or irony—sometimes all of them—collide and collaborate, and I want to reach for the phone.
I want to share the moment with my parents.

The moment is wrapped in the presence of absence.
That's the hardest day.

The hardest day is the day I want to call my parents to tell
them... something.
And more and more, what I want to tell them is a thing
about them.
Something I only understand now.
Something I didn't have the awareness or the patience
to see while they were alive and within reach.

I want my mother to know that I understand her rage now.
How it wasn't recklessness or cruelty, but a response to
being constrained, overlooked, asked to be smaller than
she was.

I want her to know that I see her brilliance—
the way her mind moved, the way she made connections,
the way she noticed what others missed.

I want her to know that what once looked like complacency
was actually choice.
A quiet, stubborn assertion of independence.
A refusal to explain herself.

These are the things I want to tell her on the hardest days.

That is grief.
Not the marked days.
Not the milestones.

The quiet, unremarkable day when understanding arrives
too late to be spoken.
That's the hardest.

five

THE THING ABOUT GRIEF IS...

nothing
is ever
the same

Especially you.

hanukkah 2023

This year, as my dad's bright light is fading,
he is surrounded by us—
his children gathered close,
keeping watch.

The house knows what is happening.
Voices soften.
Footsteps slow.
Time loosens its grip.

Even as Dad's light dims incrementally—
not all at once, but gently, faithfully—
his presence still fills the room.
His very being reminds us
not to hide in the shadows,
not to take cover in the darkness.

This is not the way he taught us to live.

Dad would never want us to dim our light.
Not now.
Not ever.

So we sit with him,
bearing witness to the leaving
and to the love that refuses to leave.

We tell stories.
We hold hands.
We keep the lamps lit longer than usual.

Hanukkah asks us to believe in small light.
In light that should not last, but does.
In flames that flicker and hold anyway.

Each night, we add another candle—
not because the darkness has receded,
but because it hasn't.
Because this is when light matters most.

My father's body is growing quieter,
but the lesson of his life is loud and clear:
Stand where you can be seen.
Offer what you have.
Shine, even when the night insists otherwise.

And so we do.

In the right light,
at the right time,
everything is extraordinary.

A hand held.
A breath taken.
A goodbye spoken softly,
wrapped in love.

And we are extraordinary too.
All of us.
Here.
Still shining.

Extraordinary.

we are carried

And when we die,
we are carried—
by those who loved us, by the stories of who we were,
by the gravity of a life that mattered.

things i carry

Over here, we don't know what happens when our dead
loved ones reach "the other side."
There is no map. No reliable witness. Only stories handed
down by the living, who are guessing.

My hope for my parents is that when they transitioned
from this world to the next,
they left behind the difficulty of their final days.
That the experiences of mottled skin, shallow breaths,
changed eye color, poor circulation, confusion,
hallucination, the inability to regulate body temperature,
the overall weakness, the death-rattle breathing—
that none of it crossed over with them.

I hope those moments loosened their grip
and fell away at the threshold.

I tell myself those final days are mine to carry.

I hold the images of their bodies betraying them.
I hold the waiting.
The counting of breaths.
The way time stretched thin and cruel.
I carry the sounds I can never unhear,
the vigilance that would not let me rest.

What I want for my parents is for them to be light—
unencumbered, unburdened,
moving through their world without the resistance of aged
joints or creaky bones.
I want them to move the way breath moves.
The way laughter does when it escapes before it's
restrained.

I want them to feel so free and so joyful
that the sun—our sun over here—
is measurably brighter because of their warmth,
their radiance bending the light.

I tell myself the discomfort of cold is mine to carry.

I hold the memory of chilled hands,
extra blankets,
socks pulled on and pulled off,
the way their bodies could no longer decide what they
needed.
I carry the ache of watching comfort become impossible.

What I want for my parents is for them to be open—
laughing, expansive,
fully who they are without the burden of who they should
have been
or how they should have shown up.
No effort.
No performance.

I want them so alive with curiosity and energy
that the blue in the sky—our blue sky over here—
is more blue because my mother's eyes are brilliant in
her full being.

I tell myself the muted ways of being are mine to carry.

I carry the restraint.
The smallness illness demanded.
The narrowing of worlds.
The conversations cut short,
the thoughts that wandered and never found their way
back.

What I want for my parents is for them to love with ease—
with a knowing of each other that no longer needs
translation or patience or repair.
I want whatever rubbed raw here
to feel irrelevant there.

I want their laughter to be so loud
that it startles us—
rattling windows,
rolling like thunder across our skies.

And if that joy requires a cost,
if that light requires weight to be held somewhere else,

I choose to hold it.

know this

What happened cannot be undone.
What is lost is lost.

I struggled with the idea of silver linings. It felt too soon,

too small, for what I was carrying. In those first months,

any attempt to brighten the loss only highlighted how
dark it felt.

I understand now that most people mean well. They want
relief for us. They want relief for themselves. They don't
know what to do with pain that doesn't improve.

But some pain doesn't improve. It deepens. It reshapes.

The way out is still through.
Through means acknowledging what hurts.
Through means not turning away.

There is nothing here to fix.
Nothing to solve.
Nothing to "move on" from.

What we need are people who can stay.
Who don't try to make it better.
Who don't insist on growth.

Some losses are not lessons.
They don't teach.
They remain.

what does not show

On this side of grief—of love, of loss—everything is altered.

There was a before, measured in breath: the steady proof
of a beating heart.
And then there was the moment the breath stopped.
The end of what was.
The beginning of what is.
The beginning of nothing ever being the same.

On this side of grief there is me—
a person who has never known a world without my mother
in it.
She was constant. Foundational.
Now she is gone.

And yet her presence is everywhere—her influence, her
voice, her way of seeing.
Everything carries her.

And she has moved on.

Nothing is ever the same.

In grief, a hole and a whole exist at the same time.
The hole she left behind.
And the whole of me—somehow both shattered and intact.

I did not know this hole before she left.
I had never examined the whole before she was gone.

Nothing is ever the same.

After my mother died, everything I did was for the first time.
The first time I went outside.
The first time I drove.
The first time I entered a public place and tried to pass
as someone whose world had not ended.

These firsts taught me where grief lives.
Not only in the big moments, but in the smallest ones.
The mundane moments—the ones that make up our days,
the ones that tether us to being human.

Grief lives in CVS.
Under fluorescent lights.
In narrow aisles lined with things meant to fix us.

It lives in standing in front of the wall of toothpaste, staring
too long.
In reaching for cotton balls or tissues or vitamins and
thinking, *Mom might need these.*
In wandering past the pharmacy counter and forgetting—
just for a second—that I am no longer picking anything
up for her.

It lives in the split second of forgetting she's dead. And
then remembering—

In the shame of that forgetting.
In the sudden heat of tears—sadness, embarrassment,
frustration, truth.

It lives in abandoning a hand basket.
In turning away from the register.
In fast-walking past greeting cards and seasonal candy,
tears spilling before I can stop them.

Nothing is ever the same.

once happy place

You know that thing people tell you to do when you're
trying to relax or fall asleep:
go to your Happy Place.

You're supposed to imagine a place of comfort and ease.
You picture the light, the air.
You let your breath slow.
Your body unclenches.
Your mind loosens its grip.
Eventually, you arrive.

My Happy Place was never imaginary.
It had a pulse.

For most of my life, it beat at the edge of the water behind
my parents' house in Islamorada.
A dock, yes—but more than that.
A rhythm.
A place that breathed with the tide.

I got married there.
I held my children there.
I taught them to look down into the water, to search for
movement—fish, rays, crabs, shadows that might become
something else.
I held their hands as they learned where to put their feet.

I held my breath as they ran—full speed, no fear—launching themselves into the Gulf as if gravity were a suggestion.

The dock held all of it.
Warmth.
Sun.
Coconut-scented skin.
Books cracked open and forgotten mid-chapter.
Towels still damp.
Laughter.
The ordinary miracle of everyone being alive at the same time.

And now.

The water keeps moving.
The light keeps striking the surface just right.
The tide does not pause to acknowledge what has changed.

The sea dares to go on.
The sun dares to shine.
The dock dares to hold its shape.

And everything is different.

Both of my parents are dead.
Most recently, my dad.

He loved that dock—maybe more than I did.

He loved to sit there and let the sun soak into him.
He loved to climb down the ladder into the water, despite
my constant fear that this would be *the* time.
It drove me fucking crazy.
He never fell.
Never got hurt.
Always wore those ridiculous waxy earplugs.

Dad believed the sea cured everything.
Because his Bubbie told him it did.
So he went in the water—to cure everything.

What the sea is curing now is unclear.

My heart is breaking in a place that keeps breathing.
The pulse is steady.
The rhythm unchanged.

My Happy Place still exists.
But I am not the same person inside it.

And for now, that is the truest thing I know.

home was never the house

I move through this place and the walls push against me.
Not literally,
but insistently, the way grief presses from all sides.

I don't know if it's the pale color, or the solid certainty
of them,
the way they keep so much in
and so much beauty out.
But I feel it.
The narrowing.
The containment.

I want to push back.

There is comfort in the way the wall meets the ceiling.
A clean seam.
A promise of order.

In this house the ceilings are high and pitched, made of
exquisite indigenous wood—
Keys cedar.
My eyes have always been drawn upward here.
In this house, I have always looked up.

I still look up.

In my imagination my parents are somewhere *up there*,
wherever that is.
I look up when I think of them.
I look up when I talk to them.
I look up when I cry out, forgetting—just for a moment—
that no answer is coming.

I look up knowing they are no longer in this house.
They are Beyond it.
Uncontained.

The walls still stand.
They remember the shape of laughter, the echo of
footsteps, the weight of ordinary days.
They hold the outline of what was.

But they cannot reach for me.
They cannot soften.
They cannot love me back.

And so I move through this place,
pressed on from all sides,
looking up—
learning the difference between shelter and home.

the void

I am in the void.

The void is not nothing.
It is the space between who I was before grief
and whoever I am expected to become next.

Before grief, life was familiar.
Repeatable.
I knew how to move through my days
without thinking about how to hold my body.
I knew the rules.

After grief—after the sting loosens—
there is a life I am not fluent in.
A life that asks me to begin again.

I don't want to be a beginner.

So I stay here.

The void is uncomfortable,
but it is a discomfort I understand.
It asks nothing of me
except honesty.
It does not rush me.
It does not require optimism.

It does not ask me to prove resilience.

The void lets me keep my parents
exactly where they are.

I know this is a choice.
I am not stuck.
I am called toward my life,
and still,
I remain.

Because I am afraid.

Afraid that moving forward means loosening my grip.
Afraid that love thins with motion.
Afraid that if I step out of this space,
the bonds will soften,
the edges will blur,
and what was sacred will become symbolic.

Afraid that I am not solid enough
to carry what comes next.

I have the language for this fear.
The tools.
The insights.
The therapists and the books and the practices.

And still,
I choose the void.

I judge myself for staying.
I judge myself for judging myself.

Grief is merciless like that.
Life too.
Death most of all.

And yet—

Here I am.
In the void.
Loving it.

Loving the ache.
Loving the closeness.
Loving the way this place still calls me by my name.

not sure yet

I'm not feeling grief.
At least not the way I think I'm supposed to.

Am I kidding myself?
Am I bypassing something essential?
Or am I feeling it—and also okay enough to sit beside the
ache without being overtaken by it?

Is that allowed?

The ease unsettles me.
The lack of drama makes me suspicious.
I judge the gentleness and suddenly it becomes clumsy,
as if grief must be heavy to be real.

Why do I do this:
measure myself against an invisible standard,
audit my own heart
to see if it's producing enough sorrow?

I keep checking in:
Is this enough grief?
Am I honoring it properly?
Am I doing this right?

Somewhere inside me lives a belief that grief should be
unmistakable—
that it should flatten me, interrupt my days, announce
itself loudly.
If it doesn't, I worry I've failed.
Or worse, that I've betrayed what I lost.

But what if grief doesn't always arrive as devastation?
What if sometimes it comes as quiet companionship,
as steadiness,
as a body that knows how to keep breathing?

What if being okay doesn't mean I've skipped the pain,
only that I've learned how to carry it without spectacle?

I'm not feeling it
and I am feeling it.
Both things are true.

And maybe the question isn't whether my grief is enough.
Maybe the question is whether I can let what *is* be
sufficient.

For now, that is enough.

i am reminded

On the day you were buried in Cleveland in mid-February, the sky was vibrant.
Blue.

Not the pale, apologetic blue of winter, but a reckless blue—clear and ringing, the kind that belongs to June. The weather hovered in the mid-60s. Cleveland in the mid-60s in February is an argument with God. It is unheard of. It is suspicious. And yet there we were, coats unbuttoned, grief sweating through wool, following quiet directions toward your burial plot.

The grandkids carried you. Wood against shoulders. Love bearing weight. I wondered, as they walked, how final a *final* resting place really is. We recited the psalm about walking through the valley of the shadow of death, our voices thin in the open air, the words drifting upward, dissolving into all that blue.

Your casket—simple, reasonable, the same color wood that lived everywhere in your Florida house—was lowered into the ground. And the sun had the audacity to keep shining. I remember feeling warm, almost hot, while the inside of me froze solid. Ice in my chest. Blue ice. I didn't want to look away as you were lowered, but I wanted to scream

at the sun, to curse the sky for its showy performance, for
its shameless beauty on the day it swallowed you.

I looked up, ready to rage.
And there you were.

The sky the same color as your eyes.
Not close. Not similar.
Exact.
That impossible, piercing blue—bright enough to stop a
room, soft enough to feel like mercy. The color that always
held me, always saw me. The color I will search for forever.

And I was reminded.

There is a place where your body—your bones—are buried.
I can give you the coordinates. Latitude and longitude. A
point on a map.
But you—
you are not contained by dirt or wood or winter ground.

You are in the blue above me.
In every impossible February sky.
Everywhere.

blue

I didn't know grief had a color until I learned it from my mother's eyes.

Blue.
Not decorative blue. Not ocean-on-a-postcard blue.
A lived-in blue. A blue that had already known loss and kept looking anyway.

When my mother looked at me, I felt seen through that blue—held in it. As though the world could bruise me and I would still be gathered back into something gentle. I didn't call it grief then. I called it love. I didn't yet understand they were the same color.

After she died, blue began to find me everywhere. In the sky when it lingered too long. In the way daylight felt too open. In the cold clarity of winter mornings. It wasn't loud. It didn't announce itself. It simply stayed.

But grief is not always blue.

Sometimes grief has no color at all.
Sometimes it drains the world until everything feels washed out—gray, thin, dimmed, as if someone turned the saturation down without asking. The reds dull. The

greens recede. Even joy arrives muted, like it has traveled too far to reach me intact.

There are days grief feels colorless, not because it is empty, but because it is too full. Too dense to name. Too heavy to see through. On those days, the world becomes a study in absence. I notice what is missing more than what remains.

And still—blue returns.

Not as spectacle.
As recognition.

Blue is the color grief uses when it wants to remind me that love once lived in a body. That it looked at me. That it had eyes. Blue is what grief wears when it is being kind.

I don't always know what to do with the color of grief. Sometimes I want to escape it. Sometimes I want to disappear into it. Sometimes I want it to leave me entirely, and other times I am afraid of a world where it doesn't find me anymore.

Blue was not new. Only my noticing was.

Love, for me, learned how to look
through blue.

guarding

I used to think grief changed my world. And it does. But more quietly, more completely, it changes the body that moves through that world. The rooms are the same size. The streets still lead where they always did. The people I love still say my name. And yet, I arrive differently.

My posture has changed.

I stand with a slight inward curve now, as if something tender lives just beneath my ribs and I am instinctively guarding it. My shoulders know a story my face doesn't tell. I hold myself like someone who has learned that loss can arrive without warning.

Grief shifts my center of gravity. I lean differently into conversations. I brace without meaning to. Laughter finds me, but it lands lower, closer to the ground. Even joy asks me to adjust my stance before I can receive it.

The hardest part isn't that relationships change. It's that I want two impossible things at once.

I want everything to be exactly how it was.
The ease. The shorthand. The way I stood without thinking.

And I want nothing to be how it was, because that body belonged to someone who had not yet learned this weight.

I want the people around me to know—by instinct—how to be with me now. To notice the way I flinch when a door closes too hard. To sense when I need space and when I need to be held in place. I want them to read my posture the way we once read each other's moods.

And when they don't, I feel the distance.

But how could they know?

I am still learning how to inhabit this body myself. I am adjusting daily to a version of me that bends where she used to stand tall, who pauses where she once rushed forward. I am asking others to love me in a stance I am still discovering.

This doesn't mean love is failing.
It means love has to renegotiate where to place its hands.

Some relationships shift easily, finding me where I am. Others reach for who I used to be and come up just short. I don't blame them. I am grieving that earlier posture too—the way I stood before I knew.

I am learning how to stand again.
This way.

i made it

I survived—and even, in some ways, thrived—to arrive at this milestone moment: the Yahrzeit of my mother, Toby Goldfinger. Yahrzeit is a Yiddish word that means *"year time"*—the anniversary of the death of a loved one—a full year with her absence walking beside me.

Along the way, I've dug in deep. I've resisted, fought with, denied, embraced, and sometimes held grief so tightly it felt like the only thing keeping me upright. People often ask what I've learned.

Here's one thing I know for sure:
Grief is not a personal growth program.

None of us need heartbreaking, confusing, life-altering loss in order to become who we are "meant to be." Life isn't transactional like that. It doesn't offer devastation in exchange for enlightenment. Life is messier—give and take, push and pull, resistance and flow. We respond to what happens. We do the best we can. No moral scoreboard. No implied lesson plan.

Loss can rearrange the world. The death of someone you love can tilt the lens through which you see everything, landing you—without consent—on the worst ride in the park, one that drops you into an unfamiliar universe while everyone else moves through their days as if nothing has changed.

I didn't need the loss of my mother to understand what matters. I didn't lose her so that something "better suited for me" could arrive in her place. I didn't need this.

And I don't have to rush to grow from it.
I don't have to put it behind me.

Life-changing events don't slip quietly away, nor do they serve as atonements for past wrongs. They change us. They become part of the terrain. What I build on top of this—more love, more depth, more wholeness—comes not from the loss itself, but from my choices. From my willingness to live in alignment with who I am and who I want to be.

Any meaning I've found inside this grief has been an act of personal sovereignty. Of self-knowledge. Chosen, not assigned.

If my mother is watching, I have a feeling she's smiling—not because I have "grown," but because I am becoming freer. More myself. Less burdened by the need to justify pain.

Mom, the presence of your absence has walked beside me for a year now, and—somehow—I am grateful for the company.

six

THE THING ABOUT GRIEF IS...

it lives with you

It doesn't pass. It participates.

deathening silence

For most of my life, I thought grief lived in tears.
In a face collapsing.
In a public moment where everyone knows what happened.

I didn't know grief could live here.

Grief is my chest tightening in a room full of laughter,
my breath shortening while everyone else breathes
without thinking.
Air goes in, but not all the way.
Something stops it halfway down.

The sound of the room is sharp—
laughter landing too close, voices brushing my skin.
My body leans back without my permission.
My shoulders lift.
My jaw locks, as if holding something in place.

The world keeps moving.
My feet stay planted in the moment everything broke.
I feel it in my legs—
heavy, rooted,
as if the floor is still asking something of me.

I laugh because my mouth remembers how.
The sound leaves me before I can stop it.

I nod. I show up.
My body performs the version of me that still fits.

Inside, something is folding inward.
Not disappearing—
contracting.
Like an organ learning it will no longer be used the same
way.

No one hears this part.
The part that holds its breath.
The part that waits.

pressing

The silence presses from the inside,
fills the space where words should land.

Sometimes the loss is quiet.
But the silence—
the silence is physical.

It crowds my chest.
It hums in my bones.
It asks my body to carry what my mouth cannot say.

reorienting

Perhaps the biggest, hardest truth of grief
is waking up and realizing I'm still here
and the world is exactly where I left it.

Nothing recalibrated.

The ground didn't tilt—
I did.

I am OK with my mom dying.
There.
I said it.

The saying of it feels worse than the truth.
It sticks in my throat.
It makes me want to apologize to people who didn't ask.

I keep waiting for the correct emotion to arrive.
The one that proves I loved her enough.

Some days I miss her so sharply I feel hollowed out.
Other days I forget to miss her at all
and that is somehow worse.

The world keeps offering me normalcy.
Conversations. Errands. Plans.
I accept them with a body that doesn't recognize itself.

I am grieving a life that no longer exists—
not dramatically,
just constantly.

My mother used to be everywhere without being noticed.
Now she is nowhere
and still everywhere.

I am learning how to be a person
who does not orbit her.
Who does not check in.
Who does not save things to tell her later.

Some days I feel strangely intact.
Functional. Almost light.

That's when the guilt shows up.
Sharp. Accusing.
As if grief should look like punishment.

Nothing feels settled.
Nothing resolves.

I am alive in a life that does not include my mother,
and I am still figuring out how to face that direction
without turning back.

headstone

My mom has been gone for almost a year and a half.
My dad for just over half a year.

Their graves are still unmarked.
No headstones.
Just earth holding what it now holds.

When I think about the markers, I don't think with words.
I feel it in my body.

A tightening.
A shallow inhale.
A pause that lasts a little too long before the exhale comes.

Somewhere inside me, I decided this was mine to do.
I live nearby.
I pass the place.
My body knows the route even when my mind avoids it.

So the task settles into me—
not as a to-do item,
but as weight.

For a long time, I carried the weight with tension.
My shoulders lifted toward my ears.
My jaw clenched.

My chest stayed guarded, as if bracing against something
sudden and sharp.

I called it procrastination.
I called it avoidance.
I let my nervous system absorb the blame.

But when I slow down enough to listen,
I hear something quieter underneath.

My body does not want to choose the moment where
breath catches.
Where the word *forever* presses down on the ribs.
Where I have to stand in one exact spot and say,
this is where the bodies are.

Even now, writing that, my breathing shifts.

Hard to breathe has a memory in me.
I watched it happen to both of my parents—
the way air became effort,
the way breath stopped being background and became
the whole story.

So of course my body resists this task.
It remembers.

Grief lives in lungs.
In the diaphragm that tightens without asking permission.

In the way the chest caves inward when something feels final.

When I hold myself more gently, I can feel another truth alongside the heaviness.
A headstone is not only an ending.
It is a place where my breath might finally settle.
A place where I don't have to hover, suspended between knowing and not knowing where to stand.

I imagine visiting without my stomach twisting.
Without my breath catching on shame.
Just standing.
Breathing.
Letting the ground meet my feet.

They were here.
Their lives moved through air and laughter and ordinary days.
And now they are held by the earth.

Today, I let my body set the pace.
I stop forcing myself through held breath and clenched resolve.
I choose to believe that when this is done, something in me will soften.

I can feel the possibility of a fuller inhale.
A longer exhale.

I can do this.
Not by pushing—
but by breathing my way toward it.

i am human

After my parents died, something else came to sit beside the grief.
It didn't announce itself.
It just lingered.

I noticed it first in my body.
A sudden heat low in my belly.
My chest tightening as if bracing for impact.
Breath turning shallow, careful.
Sometimes the room would tilt and I'd feel myself step back from the moment,
as though I'd crossed into a darker, quieter place without meaning to.

Grief was already there.
So this new presence didn't feel entirely separate.
It felt like something grief had stirred up—
something that followed me into ordinary moments.

Some days it passed quickly.
Other days it stayed, attaching itself to things I hadn't done,
things I didn't know how to do,
things that suddenly felt harder than they looked.

After loss, my capacity shrank.
I could feel it in my body before I could admit it.

Tasks took more energy.
 Decisions felt heavier.
Time moved strangely.
And when I couldn't keep up with the version of myself
I used to be,
a familiar tightening would return.

I didn't think, *I'm overwhelmed.*
I thought, *I should be handling this better.*
I didn't think, *I need support.*
I thought, *Other people manage this.*

There was a particular ache around asking for help.
As if turning outward would expose something fragile,
something already worn thin by grief.

So I carried things longer than I needed to.
I held my breath through moments that asked for softness.
I stayed silent when what I needed was company.

Only later did I begin to notice the pattern.
That this heaviness appeared right at the edge of what I
could hold alone.
That it arrived not as a verdict, but as a signal—
a quiet indication that my reach had shortened.

Grief had changed the math.
What once fit easily in my arms no longer did.

When I finally let myself lean outward—just a little—

I felt something loosen.
Not disappear.
But soften.

learning

Grief doesn't only break hearts.
It redraws the boundaries of what we can carry by ourselves.

And learning those boundaries—slowly, imperfectly—
is part of learning how to live again.

loneliness

But even in our togetherness, I wonder if the loneliness would persist.

Loneliness.

My god, this one is complicated.

The people who love me—the people who know me—want to help.

Their desire to support me is real and generous.

Some of them even understand that support doesn't mean fixing my grief or trying to usher me past it.

They sit near me.

They check in.

They use careful voices.

And still.

There is a kind of loneliness that does not come from being alone.

It comes from being the only one living inside this version of myself.

The only one whose interior landscape has been rearranged by loss.

I can be in a full room—voices overlapping, laughter moving easily—and feel a quiet distance open inside me.

Not because I don't love these people.

Not because they've failed me.
But because grief has given me a private language that
no one else is fluent in.

I nod.
I smile.
I answer questions.

Inside, I am somewhere else.

There are moments when I feel the weight of what I know
now—
how quickly bodies change,
how final certain moments are,
how fragile breath can be—
and I realize no one else in the room is holding that same
awareness in their chest.

That's the loneliness.
Not the absence of people,
but the absence of shared knowing.

Grief has made me intimate with things that don't translate
well in casual conversation.
It has slowed me down in a world that keeps moving.
It has tuned my nervous system to a frequency most
people don't hear.

So even when I am surrounded, there is a part of me
standing slightly apart,

watching,
listening,
remembering.

Sometimes I feel lonely because I don't want to bring the
room down.
Sometimes because I don't have the energy to explain.
Sometimes because the truth of where I am feels too
tender to hand over to anyone else.

i want to go home

I don't want my mom to come back because I miss her.
I want my mom to come back because having my mom
on this planet was home.

Home was the way my body softened without me noticing.
The way I didn't have to be on guard.
The way the world felt held, even when it was hard.

With her here, there was a place I could land.
A place I didn't have to earn or explain.
A place that existed simply because she did.

Now I move through the same rooms, the same streets,
the same days,
and none of them carry me in quite the same way.
Everything functions.
Nothing feels like home.

People try to offer substitutes.
Comfort.
Belonging.
Safety.

And I am grateful.
Truly.

But home is not transferable.
It is not something that can be recreated by effort or
intention.
It is something that existed quietly, until it didn't.

Without her, the world asks more of me.
I have to hold myself up in places where I used to be held.
I have to remind myself that I belong here.

I don't want her back so things can be easier.
I want her back because when she was here,
I knew—without thinking about it—
where I could rest.

That knowing is gone now.
And learning how to live without it
is my work for the rest of my days.

yearning

I'm not terrified.
I'm not even sure I'm lonely.
It seems to me that I'm yearning.

Yearning doesn't arrive with the urgency of fear or the ache of obvious sadness.
It moves more quietly.
A low hum beneath my days.
Something that leans forward inside me without telling me where it wants to go.

I feel it in my chest, not as pain exactly, but as pull.
As if some part of me is reaching for something just out of frame.
Not grasping.
Just extending.

Yearning is confusing because it doesn't name its object.
I don't always know what I want.
Sometimes it feels like a person.
Sometimes like a time.
Sometimes like a version of myself that existed before I learned certain things.

Grief sharpens yearning.
Loss clears space where longing can echo.

When someone dies, the wanting doesn't disappear with them.
It just loses its address.

So I move through the day with this quiet tilt toward something absent.
I open the refrigerator.
I step outside.
I answer messages.
All the while, a part of me is turned slightly elsewhere.

Yearning doesn't demand resolution.

It asks me to notice.

To feel how love continues to reach,
even when there is nothing left to receive it.

I'm not terrified.
I'm not lost.
I'm just standing in the space where wanting still exists,
without anywhere to land.

And somehow, that is its own kind of ache.

eliza

The last scene of *Hamilton* gutted me.
I should say the last scene guts me—still—every time.

Eliza closes the show by writing herself into the narrative,
naming the ways she shaped a country and a future, and
then she says it:
that she *had time.*

In the very last moment of the very last scene, Eliza looks
out—into the audience, into the heavens—clutching her
heart, and releases a breathy, high-pitched gasp.
I take it to be her last breath.

A small sound.
Tender.
Almost private.

An aside that matters to me: Eliza is the only character
who never raps.
Everyone else rushes.
Words tumble over one another, urgent, breathless, trying
to outrun time.

But Eliza sings.

Lin-Manuel Miranda knew what he was doing.

Eliza didn't need to hurry.
She had time.

She lived to eighty-seven.

One year more than my mom.
One year less than my dad.

For a long time, I measured my parents' lives the way
grief teaches us to measure everything—
by what ran out.
By how suddenly the time felt gone.

But that scene keeps reminding me of something quieter.

Time isn't only what ends.
It's what *opens*.

I had time with them.
Not always easy time.

Not always tender in the moment.
But time that slowly, insistently shaped my heart.

Time for ordinary days.
Time for misunderstandings and repair.
Time for love that didn't announce itself as sacred while
it was happening.

And then—after—
time to feel it.

Time to realize how much of my tenderness was learned
in their presence.
How much of my capacity to stay was practiced with them.
How even now, time keeps working—softening me,
opening me, teaching me how to hold what remains.

I didn't know I was being given something holy.
I just thought I was living my life.

Eliza's final breath isn't dramatic.
It isn't rushed.
It doesn't fight.

It simply releases.

That's what time does, eventually.
It gives us a chance to live.
And if we're lucky—
to love long enough
to become tender.

recalibrating

I have lived here all my life.
This isn't comfortable.

I know these streets—or at least I used to.
I knew which turns were automatic, which routes felt safe.
I knew how long it took to get where I was going without
checking.

Now I wake up and everything feels slightly off.
The landmarks are there, but they don't orient me.
The names have changed.
The shortcuts no longer work.

I walk through familiar places and still feel lost.
Not dramatically—just enough to notice.
Just enough to keep my shoulders tight, my attention
sharp.

Grief has altered the terrain.
It hasn't destroyed it.
It's more subtle than that.

The ground I trusted doesn't quite hold the same way.
The map in my body is outdated.
I keep reaching for reference points that no longer exist.

What unsettles me most is how ordinary this looks from the outside.
I look like someone moving through her life.
Inside, I'm constantly recalibrating.

I don't know where I am anymore,
even though I've been here forever.

And I'm learning—slowly—that this unfamiliarity isn't a mistake.
It's what happens when the place you lived was made of people.

living in relief

After my parents died, something unexpected arrived.
Space.

It wasn't gentle.
It didn't feel like freedom.
It felt like standing in a room where the machinery had
suddenly shut off,
the noise gone so fast my ears rang.

For years, my body had been trained for vigilance.
Always on.
Always listening for what might go wrong next.
Breath held just slightly above rest.

Then the emergencies stopped.
Not softened.
Not resolved.
Stopped.

The space that followed didn't feel empty at first.
It felt wrong.
Like forgetting something essential.
Like walking out of the house without keys or wallet or
phone—
a persistent sense that I'd missed my responsibility.

My nervous system stayed armed.
Even with nothing left to protect.
Even with no one left to call.

I woke up with no urgent demands and felt uneasy instead of relieved.
My body kept scanning for danger that no longer existed.
Kept reaching for pressure, for weight, for something to hold up.

When nothing arrived, I tried to fill the space myself.
With busyness.
With obligation.
With self-assigned urgency.

Anything to recreate the familiar heaviness of being needed.

It took time to realize what I was resisting wasn't emptiness.
It was relief.

Relief came in like gravity.
It dropped into my chest and stayed there.

Not the kind of relief that lifts you.
The kind that presses you down into the chair and says,
You can stop now.

Heavy relief.

The kind that makes your breath deepen without asking
permission.
The kind that loosens your shoulders so suddenly it feels
suspicious.
The kind that arrives with a quiet sense of shame,
as if ease itself needs explaining.

I loved my parents.
Caring for them consumed me.
Both are true.

Relief didn't mean I wanted them gone.
It meant my body had been holding watch for a long
time—and could finally stand down.

Standing down is not weightless.
It leaves an imprint.

There are moments when I feel the absence of urgency
more sharply than the absence of people.
Moments when the quiet feels too wide to cross.
Moments when the stillness asks more of me than the
chaos ever did.

Relief doesn't sparkle.
It settles.

It asks me to learn how to live without bracing.
Without flinching at every silence.
Without needing to justify rest.

The space is still here.
So is the sorrow.

And now I know:
relief is not the opposite of grief.
It is one of its heaviest forms.

nearer

For a long time, I thought everything I felt after loss was in the way.

The ache of being apart.
The quiet questioning of whether I was doing this right.
The moments I scolded myself for being too sad,
and the moments I scolded myself for not being sad enough.

There was guilt layered over grief,
and then guilt about the guilt.
Anger that flared unexpectedly.
Shame at myself for feeling it.

All of it felt like noise.
Like evidence that I was failing at something sacred.

So I tried to move past it.
To get to the part that was supposed to be wiser, calmer, more evolved.

But the harder I pushed, the further away that place felt.

What I'm learning—slowly—is that none of this is a detour.
The pain.
The self-doubt.

The tenderness that turns inward and bruises.

This is the path.

When I stop arguing with what's here,
when I let my heart soften instead of brace,
something unexpected happens.

I don't feel farther from the people I've lost.
I feel nearer.

Not because the pain disappears,
but because I'm no longer turning away from it.

In allowing myself to be whole—even like this,
even unfinished,
even aching—I feel a quiet closeness return.

As if love recognizes itself
in the willingness to stay.

I don't lose them by feeling all of this.
I don't lose myself.

seven

THE THING ABOUT GRIEF IS...

i can make peace with it

Healing does not have a time limit. Love blooms when the rhythm within me is peace. Beauty exists even here, even in my grief.

the body
surrenders

I'm no expert on death.
I only know what I have witnessed.

At some point—and I can't say exactly when—something shifts.

The body, which has fought so hard to stay, seems to recognize a deeper rhythm. As if it remembers something older than medicine, older than fear. The breath changes. The eyes soften. The effort gives way to something quieter.

I have sat beside more than one bed now. I have watched strong hands grow still. I have listened to the space between breaths lengthen. And each time, beneath the heartbreak, there has been a strange and humbling sense that something intelligent is unfolding—not hurried, not chaotic, but ancient.

It does not make it easier.
But it makes it feel less random.

There is a heaviness in witnessing someone leave. A weight that presses against the ribs. And there is also a lightness—not relief, not exactly—but a subtle lifting, as if

the body knows how to lay itself down when it is finished
carrying what it came here to carry.

I want to believe that this surrender is not defeat.
That it is instinct.
That the same mysterious wisdom that formed a body
knows how to un-form it.

the way forward

There is no such thing as closure.
There is no final zip, button, or snap.
We do not move on, we move with.

drying cement

Grief is dense.
Not dull—heavy.
Heavy in a way that slows everything.

Like walking through drying cement.

At first you believe you can push through it.
That if you keep moving, your body will remember what normal is supposed to feel like.
Each step costs more.
Each step asks for a strength you didn't plan to use.

Forward is what we're told to do.
Forward is what life expects.

So you move.

Moving through the world without my mother—and then without my father—was exhausting in a way I couldn't yet name.
I didn't recognize myself.
The version of me walking through the day no longer had the connection that once made movement easier.

Every task required lifting my own weight out of something that wanted to keep me.

And still, I walked.
Through the cement.

Sometimes I moved backward.
Sometimes I fell.
Sometimes I stood still and raged, because all I could
feel was the pull—
the slow grip around my legs, my chest, my breath.

I kept walking.
Not because I was brave.
Because stopping wasn't lighter.

And one day—without ceremony—the cement set.
The weight didn't leave.
Nothing lifted.
But my feet could stand.
And that was peace.

softening

My father held on as he hospiced at home for seventeen days.
Toward the end of those days his face settled into a tight, unwavering scowl.
He looked angry.
Unsettled.
As if something in him was refusing to loosen its grip.

I told myself he was angry about leaving this world.
He held on through morphine and thirst and the long absence of food.
His face barely softened.

I stayed close.
I fluffed his pillows.
Then flattened them.
Then arranged them again so the right ones rested on top of the others.
I didn't know if any of it helped him.
It helped me.

I added his favorite songs to the playlist I had made when my mother was dying.
Music filled the room.
And slowly—almost imperceptibly—his tightly balled fists began to soften.

Tiny tears gathered and slipped from the outer corners
of his eyes.

The scowl left us the night before he died.

His mouth relaxed.
His face opened.

That night, from time to time, he reached upward—
his arms lifting as if responding to something just out of
sight.
I didn't interrupt.
I didn't ask.

I told myself he was reaching for his people.
For those who had gone before him.
Maybe even for the animals he loved.

It was devastating.
And it was beautiful.

He didn't say anything that night.
But something in him changed.

Watching him, I learned that dying is not always giving up.
Sometimes it is a softening.
Sometimes it is a release that doesn't look like relief,
but like surrender to what has always been waiting.

And I stayed.

both/and

I can be both sadness and wonder.

Sadness sits in my chest.
It's thick.
It doesn't move much.

It knows the names I still say.
It knows the empty weight of rooms after people are gone.

Wonder doesn't come to help.
It doesn't smooth anything out.
It shows up without asking—
a strip of light,
a breath I didn't plan on taking.

They don't alternate.
They don't correct each other.

Sadness stays heavy.
Wonder stays tender.

I carry them.

beauty as an ally

Beauty exists even here, even in my grief.

I say that carefully, because for a long time I believed beauty required permission.
As if noticing the way the light falls across the floor meant I was forgetting you.
As if letting my breath soften meant I was moving on too quickly.
As if grief demanded a posture—head down, eyes dimmed, joy withheld—until some invisible authority declared me finished.

But grief is not a vow of ugliness. It is not a contract that says I must avert my eyes from what is still alive.

The world did not stop being beautiful when you died.
The sky did not dim itself out of respect.
Trees continued their quiet labor.
Water kept moving.
Beauty kept happening without consulting my pain.

At first, this felt cruel.
How dare the world go on being so lovely when my heart had been split open?
How dare I notice it?

And then, slowly, something else began to emerge.

What if beauty is not the opposite of grief?
What if it is one of the ways grief breathes?

I am still broken, and the morning light is still beautiful.
Both are true.
I miss you with a ferocity that startles me, and I am moved
by the way the air smells after rain.
Neither cancels the other.
Neither needs to be justified.

There is a quiet lie that grief tells us:
that suffering must be constant to be legitimate.
That relief is suspicious.
That moments of ease are a kind of betrayal.

But grief is not measured by how little beauty we allow in.
Love does not require us to stay clenched forever.

When I let beauty in now, it does not take me away from
you.
It brings me closer.
Because beauty reminds me that I am still capable of
feeling.
That my heart, though wounded, is not sealed shut.
That something in me remains tender enough to notice.

I do not owe my sorrow an apology for moments of light.
I do not owe the world a performance of endless sadness.

I am allowed to stand in beauty and still carry you with me.

Beauty exists here.
Not as an escape.
Not as a solution.
But as a companion.

And staying with it—without guilt, without explanation—
does not mean I have left my grief behind.
It means I am still alive inside it.

peace

I say it to myself when the ground inside me won't stay still.
I am peace.

Not because I feel peaceful.
Not because the grief has softened or loosened its grip.
But because something in me knows that peace does
not require quiet.

Grief is loud.
It stirs. It disrupts. It pulls at the nervous system like
weather.
It arrives without asking and rearranges the furniture.
And still—
I am peace.

Peace, I am learning, is not the absence of sorrow.
It is the willingness to let sorrow move without being exiled.
It is the decision to stay present even as the heart trembles.
It is breath that continues even when the chest is tight.

There are days when my inner world feels like a shaken
snow globe—
memories rising, emotions colliding, everything suspended
and unsettled.
On those days, peace does not look like stillness.
It looks like allowing the storm to pass through me

without deciding it means something has gone wrong.

I am peace does not cancel my grief.
It holds it.

It means I do not abandon myself when the sadness
surges.
I do not rush to fix or resolve or explain it away.
I let grief speak in its own language—
through tears, through exhaustion, through longing—
and I remain here, listening.

This is what happens when I stop resisting what is already
true.
When I let my body carry what it knows how to carry.
When staying becomes the only requirement.

Peace lives in the choice to soften my jaw
even while my heart aches.
It lives in the way I place a hand on my own body
as if to say, *I'm here. You don't have to go anywhere.*

I am not peaceful because my life is orderly.
I am peaceful because I am no longer at war with my grief.

The chaos still comes.
The waves still rise.
But beneath them, there is a deeper current—
steady, quiet, unchanged.

That is where peace lives.
Not above the grief.
Not beyond it.
But within me, alongside it.

I am peace.
Even here.
Especially here.

lovingly placed

I've been in this place more times than I can count.
Weeks at a time.
Months, even.

But this time is different.
Not because the house has changed—
because I have.

I look around more slowly now.
As if the room is speaking in a language I finally understand.

This is where I was married.
On the dock.
The sun lowering itself into the water as if it knew to
witness us.

This is also where my parents took their last breaths.
Same place.
Same air.
Life arriving and leaving without asking permission.

And now I am here for the last time.
And for the first time, I am noticing.

Not the house—
the intention.

Everywhere I look, there is evidence of care.
My mother's care.
Not loud. Not ornamental.
But precise.

Colors chosen, not by trend, but by feeling.
Blues that calm.
Greens that steady.
Pinks that soften what might otherwise feel too sharp.

Nothing accidental.
Nothing rushed.

I run my eyes across the room and can feel her pauses.
Her deciding.
Her quiet satisfaction when something felt *just right*.

My father is here too.
Not in the way people say someone "lingers."
But in usefulness.
In repetition.

Photographs of fish caught and trips taken.
The wall of fishing rods, each one placed as if it mattered
where it rested.

They didn't just live here.
They *meant* things here.

And now I understand—

this is what we are left with.

Not stuff.
But evidence.

Evidence of who they were when no one was watching.
Evidence of what they valued.
Evidence of love expressed sideways, through choices
and placement and care.

It weaves itself into memory, yes—
but also into the ordinary things we touch and see and
move past every day.

a place is not
a person

I have so many memories.
They are mine.

During the final walk-through of the house,
I move slowly, as if speed might undo something.
My hand drifts along the walls,
not because I think they will remember me,
but because I am not yet ready to stop remembering here.

Grief makes everything feel fragile.
As if love could be misplaced.
As if leaving might mean abandoning what mattered.

But a house doesn't get to hold what is dear to me.
A house is not a person with a memory.
It cannot miss us when we are gone.
It cannot carry love forward.

The walls witnessed a life.
They stood nearby while it happened.
That is all.

The memories don't live here.
They live in me.

They live in the way my body hesitates in the doorway.
In the way my chest tightens before the key turns.
In the way my heart knows this moment matters,
even if nothing visible is changing.

I check the rooms one last time.
Nothing is missing.
Nothing has been forgotten.

When I lock the door,
I do not leave my people behind.

What I loved comes with me—
carried in the only place it has ever lived.

When the lock clicks,
nothing essential stays in the house.

the middle path

Some days I have one foot in the room where you are gone
and one foot in the room where the world keeps going.
And the stretch between them burns.

The middle path sounds spiritual. Balanced. Wise.
But it doesn't feel that way from here.

It feels like standing in the danger zones of my own life
and not running.

It feels like wanting to collapse into the ache
or bolt toward anything that makes me forget—
and choosing neither.

The middle path is neither on nor off.
It's not "moving on."
It's not staying loyal to my devastation.

It's staying with myself
while everything I knew rearranges.

There is no shortcut.
No secret door marked redemption.
No moment where grief politely steps aside and says,
"You've suffered enough. You may pass."

Instead there is this:

The empty space at the table.
The sudden punch of memory.
The ordinary Tuesday that doesn't know it has been split
in two.

The middle path asks me to turn toward all of it.
Not to dramatize it.
Not to numb it.
Just to feel it without leaving my own body.

Standing here, inside this obliterated universe,
I am shocked to find my heart still beating.

Somehow I make a home.

Not by choosing to be "OK" and leaving you behind.
Not by clinging to you so tightly I refuse to live.

I don't have to prove my love by staying broken.
I don't have to betray my love by healing.

The middle ground is not glamorous.
It is messy and ordinary and sometimes unbearably quiet.

It lets me love you
and keep breathing.

It lets grief widen me
without swallowing me whole.

And I don't always walk it well.
But I stay.

not a funny thing

It's a strange not-strange thing that continues as I write about grief and loss and death.

I want my writing about death to live.
I want it to breathe.
I want readers to feel opened by it—not buried.

I want to say that death, loss, grief—this most universal human experience—can widen us into the best parts of who we are.

And at the very same time—

There is a slideshow I cannot turn off.

While I write about love, about light, about sacredness, another reel runs beneath the words.

My mother's fixed gaze.
The way her mouth stayed open when there was no more breath.
My father's blue-grey mottled skin, the map of his body changing hour by hour.
The smell of sickness that clung to the sheets.
The sound—that sound—of dirt and rock striking the top of the casket.

Thud.
Then another.

I can be mid-sentence, writing about beauty, and suddenly I am back in the room. Standing next to the hospital bed. Back in the hospice silence that was anything but silent. The death rattle. The antiseptic. The sweetness of flowers trying and failing to cover what was happening.

It lives in my body.

Every word I have written carries weight. Not metaphorical weight. Physical. My jaw tightens. My stomach turns. My chest constricts. I have had to move images aside—not to deny them—but to make enough space inside myself to write about what was also true.

Because alongside the wasting bodies, there was devotion. Alongside the smells and sounds, there was tenderness. Alongside the casket, there was love so fierce it still hums in my bones.

I could not write about grief and loss and death head on. If I stared only at the ghastly images, I would freeze there.

So I turn slightly.
Not away.
Just enough to breathe.

I will never be without those final days.

They come uninvited.
They interrupt beauty.
They sit behind every paragraph.

And still, I am here.
Still, I am OK.

the pain is clean

Grief is not something I cradle.
It sits on me.

A weight—
not crushing,
but certain.
Like a stone placed at the center of my chest by hand.

It does not glow.
It does not teach.
It does not arrive with wisdom.

It is simply the fact
that you were here
and now you are not.

Some days I press into it the way a tongue finds the
broken edge of a tooth.
Not to hurt myself.
Just to feel where the nerve still lives.

The pain is clean.
Cleaner than the forced brightness of "moving on."
Cleaner than the applause people offer when I appear
functional.

Grief does not blur you.
It refuses to let your outline soften.
The exact tilt of your head.
The way your silence filled a room more fully than anyone
else's voice.
The empty chair that is not symbolic—
it is just empty.

I keep my grief close because it is the only place where
you remain undiluted.
Out in the world, you become a story.
A photograph.
A past tense.

In grief,
you are still dimension and heat.

Letting go would not be brave.
It would be erasure.

So I stay.

Not stuck.
Not saintly.
Not performing resilience.

I am happy to be sad—
not because sadness is beautiful,
but because it is honest.

It does not pretend you mattered less than you did.
It does not reduce you to something I survived.

This ache is proof of scale.
Of depth.
Of attachment that did not evaporate when your body did.

I am not healed.
I am not broken.

I am in an ongoing relationship
with someone the world insists is gone.

And I will not make that relationship smaller
for the comfort of anyone else.

because i love me

Because I love me,
I can love that my experience of grief is difficult.

Because I loved you,
I can accept that it was your time to move on.

Because I love me,
I am willing to explore the strangeness of this new world—
the one where you are gone and I am still here.

Because I love me,
I can walk through a crowded room
and admit I feel completely alone.

Loving me means I do not abandon myself
inside that loneliness.

You loved me first.
You showed me what it felt like to be seen—
in your eyes, in your steadiness, in the way you stayed.
And even if I had doubted it,
I would still be here now, learning to love myself anyway.

Because I love me,
I keep going.

Because I love me,

I make decisions I never wanted to make.

There are moments I have felt guilt about the timing of
your death.
Moments I have wondered if I did too much,
or not enough.

But because I love me,
I remember this:

You were dying.
Your body was finished.
There was no more light left for it to hold.

We did not force the ending.
We witnessed it.

On a clear, starry night,
with all of us gathered close,
you took your final breath.

Because I love me,
I can live with that memory
without turning it into a weapon against myself.

Because I love me,
I can love the shift grief creates—
even when I don't like it.

Because I love me,
I stay.

epilogue

Here is what I know now.
Say their name.

Say it when it rises in your throat and presses against
your teeth.
Say it even when the sound of it drops you to your knees.
Especially then.

Let other people say their name too.
Let them bring you stories—small offerings—the way your
person once carried tissues in a pocket or left lollipop
wrappers in a sweatshirt.
Let remembering matter more than comfort.

You will find them in the ordinary relics.
A grocery list.
A coat pocket.
The shape of their handwriting.
You will laugh when you didn't expect to.
Let that happen.

Breathe.
And then breathe again.

When grief comes like a tide, don't argue with the water.
Let it pull you under if it must.
Let the sobs move through you until something unclenches.
You are not weak for this.
You are loving.

The world will keep spinning.
It is not doing this to wound you.
Still, it may feel like it is.

You are altered now.
Every part of you has been rearranged by love and by loss.

Let go of what asks to be released.
Let go of people who cannot stay.
Take the time you take.
There is no calendar for sorrow.
Grief does not respond to deadlines.

Speak what needs to be spoken.
Hold what feels sacred.
Create room for remembering.
Create room for laughter.
Create room for both.

You will feel alone.
You will not be alone.

This is not a blessing.
It is an invitation.

Make a life that can hold your grief and still call it beautiful.

acknowledgments

This book was written in the aftermath of loss, and in the presence of people and one dog who made it possible to stay.

To those who allowed me to speak about my parents, to say their names out loud, to tell the same stories more than once—thank you for listening without trying to make it better. Your willingness to sit with me, just as things were, made more difference than you know.

David, thank you for your steadiness. For staying when I felt unmoored, for making room for both grief and this book, and for the quiet ways you reminded me that life was still here.

To my sons Sam and Gabriel, who have built lives of their own while carrying forward the love that shaped them—you are part of what remains, and part of what continues.

To Heather Doyle Fraser and the production team at Compassionate Mind Collaborative (Hope Madden, Cindy Curtis-Rivera, and Jesse Sussman), your work gave language to what I was living—your words met me in moments when I could not find my own. Your reflections now live within these pages and on its cover.

To the early readers (Jacob Nordby, Mark J. Silverman, Rev. Rachel Hollander, Steve Chandler, Patti M. Hall, Jason Goldberg, Bay LeBlanc Quiney, and Chris Fraser) who met this book and offered their words—thank you for your care, your attention, and your willingness to stand beside this work. There is a particular vulnerability in being read this way, and I am deeply grateful for the way you met it.

To the clients and leaders I've had the privilege to work with: you trusted me with your stories, your losses, and your humanity. This book is shaped, in part, by what you have allowed me to witness.

To David Kessler, and my grief colleagues who helped me understand grief not as something to solve, but as something to live with—thank you for expanding the way I see, listen, and remain.

And to Mimsy, whose joyful presence made space for both grief and words, and who reminds me daily how to stay.

Because grief is already here, and endings will always arrive, I am still learning to stay.

about the author

KAREN GOLDFINGER BAKER

Karen Goldfinger Baker is an executive and leadership coach whose work explores the intersection of loss, grief, and trauma. Trained at the Weatherhead School of Management at Case Western Reserve University and credentialed by the International Coaching Federation and EMCC Global, she works with leaders from companies including Amazon, Apple, Facebook, Google, Oura, and Zendesk, as well as retired professional athletes.

Karen is trained in trauma and somatics and is a Certified Grief Educator in partnership with David Kessler. She is also the host of *Stay Here* and *Trauma Hiders Club*, both of which explore how we carry what life gives us.

She lives with her husband, David, and their Giant Schnauzer, Mimsy, who reminds her daily how to stay.